Praise for *The Barefoot Executive*

"There has never been a better time to turn your passions into income. But just having an idea doesn't mean you're ready to order business cards just yet. Carrie Wilkerson's *The Barefoot Executive* walks you through the process of developing your idea, finding your audience, and setting yourself up for a lifetime of success doing the work you love for the hardest boss you'll ever have—yourself!"

> — Dave Ramsey, host of *The Dave Ramsey Show* and best-selling author of *The Total Money Makeover*

"A lot of books can fire up an entrepreneur. But a lot of those books leave readers high and dry when it comes to practical application. Enthusiasm isn't enough. You need a plan and the tools to build with. Carrie Wilkerson's guidance provides just that. Combine that with her enthusiasm, warmth, and core values, and you have someone very real to learn from. As my dad says, 'a great book needs to cover the Why and the How.' This *is* a great book. I know that when Carrie advises Ziglar, Inc., on marketing ideas, we get results. "

> — Tom Ziglar, CEO, and proud son of Zig Ziglar.

"One of the best ways to achieve success is to learn from someone who has already done it. If you are looking to build a viable, sustainable, and lucrative business from home—or anywhere else—Carrie Wilkerson is your example, and her new book will show you the way."

> — Tim Sanders, author of *Today We Are Rich* and former CSO at Yahoo!

"If I'd had this book in hand a few years ago, it would have saved me countless hours of valuable time. Do yourself a favor and absorb the lessons learned here."

> — Chris Brogan, president, Human Business Works, and publisher of chrisbrogan.com

"Packed with real-world case-studies, action items, business models and links to free coaching videos, *The Barefoot Executive* isn't just a book, it's a multimedia roadmap that takes you by the hand and walks you down the road to earning a living on your terms and reclaiming ownership of your life."

— Jonathan Fields, author of *Career Renegade*

"If you're dreaming of building a business on your terms, then you'll absolutely love Carrie Wilkerson."

— Tory Johnson, CEO, Women For Hire, and *New York Times* best-selling author

"*The Barefoot Executive* is the kind of book every entrepreneur or hopeful small business owner should read, regardless of their gender or age. It's packed with practical wisdom and advice to help you turn ideas into actions and actions into results."

— Jon Gordon, international best selling author of *The Energy Bus*

"If you're dreaming of a life beyond the nine-to-five grind, if you want real financial security, if you want to be the CEO of your own life, read *The Barefoot Executive*. Author Carrie Wilkerson offers real-life advice on finding or creating a *profitable* business model that works for you."

— Erin K. Casey, books editor, *SUCCESS magazine*

"The powerful connection Carrie makes with her audience members from stage is duplicated in this terrific book. You feel like you're sitting one-on-one with your trusted friend and mentor, and she is simply sharing with you everything she knows about building a hugely successful business. The cool thing is, not only has she done it but also she will show you how to do the same!"

— Bob Burg, coauthor of *The Go-Giver* and *Endless Referrals*

"Forget getting a job—go out and make one! That's right, your best chance for long-standing life security lies in running your own business—one where your unique strengths meet the needs of the marketplace. *The Barefoot Executive* shows you how to make that happen. Not only a great business example, Carrie's model of keeping her priorities in order while creating an amazing life is an inspiration to anyone who feels like they need to choose between a life or a business. She shows you can succeed in the business we are all in—the Business of Life! A giver who is passionate about helping those in need, Carrie is truly fueled by how much she can give and do for others. Read this, be inspired, then take action."

— Frank McKinney, bestselling author
of *The Tap;* www.The-Tap.com

"Few people in the world would I consider True Leaders, and ever fewer would I consider to have a genius for what they do. Carrie Wilkerson does. Her new book, *The Barefoot Executive*, is one amazing work, and if you are in the marketplace working, you need to read this amazing book. It is so powerful they are going to have to issue WARNING labels with it as it is deadly to your mediocrity. Brilliant. Powerful. Genius."

— Doug Firebaugh, CEO, PassionFire
International

"If you read nothing but Part 2 of *The Barefoot Executive*, you will save yourself years of frustration and countless dollars."

— John Jantsch, author of *Duct Tape
Marketing* and *The Referral Engine*

"In true Carrie Wilerson style, she explains the importance of the 'how' and the steps of the 'how' through the filter of your 'why.' I believe this is what sets Carrie apart from all others and why she is number 1. I was in the middle of a 3.5 million dollar product launch and got stuck . . . I knew exactly who to call for the answers: Carrie Wilkerson. Asked, answered, success."

— Paul Martinelli, PaulMartinelli.net

"In an age where so many claim to be experts, Carrie Wilkerson is a breath of fresh air. She doesn't just talk the talk, she has actually walked the walk! She has built successful businesses while raising a young family, overcoming extreme debt, and generating funds and awareness of orphan and adoption issues. She has experienced firsthand the difficulties entrepreneurs face on a daily basis and shares openly the strategies, tactics, and tools she uses to overcome those challenges and generate executive income businesses. With her energetic spirit and passion for helping others, Carrie has rapidly become the go-to person for anyone wanting to grow—and sustain—their business in today's volatile marketplace."

— Wendy Kurtz, APR, CPRC

"*The Barefoot Executive* is a must-read for aspiring entrepreneurs or established business owners who want to take their business to the next level. Carrie shares the proven strategies she has used for years to create several six-figure businesses. If you're serious about creating and growing a business, you need this book."

— Lisa Kanarek, author and founder
of WorkingNaked.com

"In a world of questionable work-from-home advice, Carrie Wilkerson brings a breath of fresh air, integrity, solid tools, and valuable business savvy. She has created enormous personal and financial success by following her own advice. If you want to step off the corporate treadmill, be present for your family, and earn a great living, you need to read this book."

— Pamela Slim, author of *Escape from
Cubicle Nation*

"At a time when pseudo-experts are overwhelming us with unproven theories and regurgitated ideas, Carrie Wilkerson shines like a beacon in the night. Not only has she built a successful business of her own, but she's proven that she can teach others to do the same. In *The Barefoot Executive*, Carrie offers a clear roadmap to defining and building an amazing life on your own terms. I particularly like the practical exercises throughout the book. Read it . . . and then go do it."

— Paul Keetch, author of *Make My
Marketing Work*

"This book is really strong. It provides the why and how to be your own boss. The tips and the case studies give actionable steps and examples of how it has worked for others. We deal with so many people that want out of their current job situation due to the work, lack of challenge, desire for more family time, or a passion for something specific. They don't know what to do or how to go about doing their own thing. We have started doing a number of educational programs just to help people gain the knowledge to be in business before we try to help them one on one. This book is a great guide. It provides clear advice and how to make the jump to business ownership from 'how do I decide what to do' to 'how do I do it?' I think you have a winner here!"

— Michael Bowers, Ohio Small
Business Development Center

"Starting a business can be intimidating and even a bit frightening. Among other things, Carrie provides four proven (and realistic) online models to get you going. Plus with her stern but loving style you'll get the confidence you need at the right time to create a vision for what's really possible."

— Yanik Silver, author of
Moonlighting on the Internet

"Once in a while we meet those amazing people who not only reach great heights in their own lives, but who also inspire others to achieve greatness. Carrie Wilkerson is one of those people. *The Barefoot Executive* is the ultimate how-to for anybody trying to write their own success story. It gives the tools, the insights, the wisdom and the heart to have it all—but mostly the tools! That is what we need. The author lays out a roadmap and literally guides the reader through the woods and weeds and out into the sunlight of success . . . This is how you get from here to there!"

— Mary Agnes Antonopoulos, social
media strategist

"Carrie's brilliant entrepreneurial strategies will teach you how to identify and develop your ideas and how to promote those ideas to their greatest potential success."

— Sally Hogshead, author of
*Fascinate: 7 Triggers to Persuasion
and Captivation*

"Carrie Wilkerson knows what it takes to start and grow a successful business, and she generously shares it ALL in this book. As important, she focuses on helping entrepreneurs craft a plan that supports their values—the secret to meaningful success. You can do it, and Carrie will show you how!"

— Keith Ferrazzi, best-selling author
of *Never Eat Alone*

The
BAREFOOT
EXECUTIVE

The

BAREFOOT EXECUTIVE

The ULTIMATE GUIDE *for*
Being Your Own Boss
& Achieving Financial Freedom

CARRIE WILKERSON

THOMAS NELSON
Since 1798

NASHVILLE   DALLAS   MEXICO CITY   RIO DE JANEIRO

Published in Nashville, Tennessee, by Thomas Nelson. Thomas Nelson is a registered trademark of Thomas Nelson, Inc.

Thomas Nelson, Inc., titles may be purchased in bulk for educational, business, fund-raising, or sales promotional use. For information, please e-mail SpecialMarkets@ThomasNelson.com.

This book is intended to provide accurate information with regard to the subject matter covered. However, the Author and the Publisher accept no responsibility for inaccuracies or omissions, and the Author and Publisher specifically disclaim any liability, loss, or risk, whether personal, financial, or otherwise, that is incurred as a consequence, directly or indirectly, from the use and/or application of any of the contents of this book.

Library of Congress Cataloging-in-Publication Data

Wilkerson, Carrie, 1972–
    The barefoot executive : the ultimate guide for being your own boss and achieving financial freedom / Carrie Wilkerson.
        p. cm.
    Includes bibliographical references and index.
    ISBN 978-1-59555-369-0
    1. New business enterprises—Management. 2. Entrepreneurship. I. Title.
HD62.5.W489 2011
658.1'1—dc22   2011014384

Printed in the United States of America

11 12 13 14 15 QGF 5 4 3 2 1

To Eddie, Mark, Emily, Catie, and Lily—my reasons "why"

Contents

Introduction

On these pages you won't read how I've been a business owner since birth or sold Beanie Babies on eBay, predicting my entrepreneurial destiny.

I have never operated a lemonade stand. I didn't have a paper route. I wasn't required to help my parents put food on the table, and honestly, I never gave going into business for myself a second thought.

After getting a high school education, attending college to study music (which I abandoned for marriage, choosing to finish a degree that took fewer hours and less time away from my beloved), I still was set on a course of traditional employment. More specifically, I was employed in a government-run educational institution.

Yes, I was a teacher. And I loved it. I thought I would be teaching for a long while.

And then I became a mother. The story leading up to it perhaps isn't so important to you, but the end result is that I was a mother of toddler siblings and my priorities shifted more quickly than the ink on the adoption papers dried.

I was a mother. My kids needed me. And for various reasons, I wasn't going to leave them in the care of someone else if I could figure out how to avoid it.

However, I had no financial plan. I had no savings account. We relied on my salary as my husband was still climbing the corporate ladder. But it was what it was, and we had six weeks left of a teacher's summer paycheck to figure something out.

That was in 1998, and I have since rendered myself—and now even my husband—unemployable. We cannot and will not consider working on a schedule, on a time clock, or on a payroll for anyone else.

We now have four children and live a life of financial independence and what I would consider full security—meaning, we are dependent only on our ability to serve our clients and offer value to the marketplace.

This is what I want for you.

I don't have a business degree. I've never taken a certified business class or been "credentialized" in any formal way. My advice is from real application, practical techniques, and solid experience. From babysitting and bagging groceries for tips to being a barefoot CEO, we really are in a time when we can create our own realities. No longer do we rely on a standard track of education, then apply for a job, stay until we retire, and pray for security and good benefits along the way. We really are in a position to create our own careers, our own paths, and our own incomes, if we dare.

My goal is to give you hope and to take you through the process of investigating your options and your skill sets to create the financial freedom and work life that you've perhaps only dreamed of until now.

Ignore the naysayers and avoid the status quo.

What Are Your Motives?

Why do you want to start a business? Why are you reading this book?

- Are you looking for a fortune or are you looking for a legacy?
- Are you looking to make money?
- Are you chasing cash or are you trying to build a sustainable business?

Money is never enough. The money will never, ever be enough.
The "why" behind the money, the "why" behind how you are changing

people, the "why" behind what you do is what you are really focused on. And again, that may evolve.

When I started working at home in 1998, it was because we had adopted two toddlers and overnight, literally, I had become a mom. We had twenty-four to thirty-six hours to prepare. I was teaching high school at the time and really loved it, but this adoption adjusted my priorities instantly.

I did not start my business because I had a big passion for what I was doing, because I was chasing a big idea, or because I wanted to make big money. I started my business because I refused to leave my children in the care of someone else. I didn't want them to question who their mom was and, frankly, I still needed a paycheck. Period.

I didn't want them to wonder if they were in the right place. I didn't want them to suffer one more moment of neglect in their lives. I purposed in my heart that I would be there, no matter the sacrifice. So, I walked away from a career that I loved and chose to work at home. The work-at-home climate at that point was not as user-friendly as it is now. There were not as many things to do. We were not as technologically connected. But I was determined to make something work.

I was there for all that time with my children and I'm happy to report they are very well-adjusted, amazing children. They have no doubt who loves them and who their momma and daddy are because we have been here with them.

We've added two children the old-fashioned way since we have been working at home.

My "why" has evolved over the years. My "why" evolved to getting out of debt. And then it evolved to bringing my husband home from a corporate job because he was traveling so much and missing us so much and missing so much of the kids' lives.

Now that we are financially stable and the kids are a little older and very secure in who they are and my husband is home working with us, now my "why" is you. You are a huge part of what drives me. I want you to be able to experience what we have experienced. I want you to feel the financial freedom to get out of debt, to not be in bondage to an employer, and to give generously and joyfully to causes you are passionate about, as we do for orphan care and adoption.

The number of dollars I earn does not propel me. The number of children I can help and the number of opportunities for my children and for my family propel me. I have a son with extensive special needs, and to be able to shop for therapies and treatments based on what is best rather than by price tag is—well, it's priceless. Those are the kinds of choices I want for your family too.

So, when I say the money is never enough, what I mean is you are never going to work really hard just to have a lot of money. Money is intangible and is not really at its very core anything that really motivates us. What motivates us is what the money can do or the cause it can support or the choices that money allows us to have. You want to be rich in what? Rich in blessing, rich in opportunities, rich in choices, rich in freedom, rich in what? I want you to really think about your "why."

Your Turn

What will drive you to get out of bed, to skip that TV show, to push a little harder? Write a few of those why's down before we get any further.

_____

_____

_____

A Map

This is how I built several six-figure businesses—and beyond—over and over again, using the same format and formula. We wouldn't start a house without a plan, without a design, without a blueprint, so I wonder why so many of us jump into business without any structure, any plan, or any advisement.

Even if you are established in business, even if you are profitable in business, and even if you have done this before, I know you are going to have an "Aha!" moment or be reminded of something valuable to you that you haven't thought of in a while.

I've overcome more than $100,000 worth of commercial debt, lost more than one hundred pounds, I'm raising four children at home, and I have done all of this while building businesses—not in a corporate structure, not in an office, not in a storefront, but out of my home.

If I can do that using these formulas, I know that no matter what your business model, your situation, your market, your niche, or whatever you want to do, you can apply this too.

Please be open-minded. Don't say, "That won't work for me because *xyz*." Be open, and know that I've been there and done that and I want what is best for you and what is best for your business.

Let's consider the first question, which is always "What can I do?"

"Carrie, what can I do from home?"

- What can I do to earn some extra money part-time?
- What can I do to build a business full-time?
- What can I do that isn't already done to death?
- What can I do and keep my values intact?

We all have to ask ourselves those questions. Sometimes it is a matter of "I'm professionally trained as an attorney or a CPA or a teacher." Maybe you are a nurse, trained in the medical field, but what else could you do?

We are going to talk about some ways you could think a little differently.

- Maybe you've been at home with your children or taking care of your parents or doing something else, and you have been out of the workforce a really long time.
- Maybe you've never had to work.
- Maybe you are deciding whether or not to go to college or to school or to vocational training.

Even if you have an established business but you are looking for another stream of income, I encourage you to ask that question: What can I do?

We are going to talk about business models—some idea prompters for you. We are also going to talk about multiple income streams, profit streams, income sources—however you want to label those—in your existing business.

I have heard a lot of people say, "Do what you love and the money will follow." I don't necessarily agree. I believe you should be passionate first about profitability and then your skill set will yield profits that fund your passion.

My basic plan starts with some evaluations:

Evaluate Your Space: The first thing I always recommend that you do is look at your space. What kind of space do you have available?

Evaluate Your Skills: What skill set do you already have?

Evaluate Your Software: What kind of software do you have? What kind of software have you been trained to use? What are you willing to learn?

Evaluate Your Service: What are you already being paid for or what have you been paid for in the past? Were you a teacher? Were you a nurse? Did you provide child care? Have you cleaned homes? Were you a secretary? Have you done phone work?

I believe that no matter what you've done in the past, no matter what your skill set has been, there is a way to take either what you've done in the past or what you are currently doing and translate that into part-time or full-time income.

Many times we get so frustrated with the position we are in that we want to do something radically different. That is not always the fastest path to profitability. Often the fastest route to profitability is paddling downstream, meaning to go with the flow of what you know. Let's profit from that first. Then when you are good and profitable and you get it to cash, you can start pursuing some of the things you are passionate about.

I don't know about you, but I am pretty passionate about paying the bills and making sure we have food and clothing and our necessities covered. Get passionate about getting to the place of profitability. Then you can pursue some things that you are interested in.

Perhaps I'm getting ahead of myself. I have been accused of talking (and typing) faster than I think—so let's get started with some fairy tales before we get to the happily ever after.

How to Get the Most out of This Book

I don't really consider this a textbook or a "how-to" guide in the traditional sense. I'm not sure I'd recommend reading it start to finish or in one sitting. Perhaps this is a book that you need to keep handy and refer to again and again as you reach different points in your journey to self-employed freedom.

Are you still working full-time and wanting to transition to working at home? Then you should start at the beginning and read with a highlighter and pad of sticky notes in your hand for the overview, making note of the pages you want to revisit later as the information sinks in.

Are you already in a business? Then you can flip to the chapters on getting more clients and creating new streams of income within your business model. There's really no need for you to do discovery on what you should be doing if you are already profitable.

Barefoot Action Steps

I've included brief Barefoot Action Steps in chapters 1 through 16. These are brief "diligence devotionals," if you will. In a few minutes I educate you, encourage you, and give you food for thought as you pursue your dreams. Each Barefoot Action Step contains a Web address for a video created just for my readers. Enjoy the video before you read each Action Step.

Barefoot Case Studies

Maybe you are a chronic starter or endless struggler and you just need some encouragement. That's included in these pages too. As a matter of fact, this book is peppered with Barefoot Case Studies of friends, colleagues, and clients who have designed their lives and their businesses on their own terms. They range from five- to seven-figure businesses, from professionals to kitchen-table setups, and from service to information to Internet marketing and everything in between. Let these men and women inspire you. My story may not resonate with you at all. But I guarantee that one of these men or women will have something in common with you and will encourage you to keep on keeping on. Read carefully as they tell their stories in their own words. You will be amazed and motivated, as I always am.

I encourage you to find a way to use this book to your advantage. If you started with the Introduction, return to the Contents page. From there you can decide where you are in the process—and where you want to begin. Use this book to think differently, to work smarter, to develop deeper, and to become the independent soul that you crave to be.

BAREFOOT ACTION STEP

What Are You Waiting For?

Waiting is a trap. There will always be reasons to wait. The truth is, there are only two things in life, reasons and results, and reasons simply don't count.

—Dr. Robert Anthony

Watch the "What Are You Waiting For?" video at http://barefootexecutivevideos.com/waiting

I want to talk to you about something that may or may not seem obvious or intuitive to you, but it is something that I see a lot as a business consultant and strategist and also see a lot in the marketing space. People are so worried about the big idea, the grand idea, the million-dollar idea, that they are overlooking all the hundred-dollar ideas or thousand-dollar ideas or hundred-thousand-dollar ideas.

Quit worrying about getting it perfect, getting it right, and getting rich the first time. You can absolutely build freedom and create wealth ten, twenty, and one hundred dollars at a time. I'm proof of that. I started with a $35 per month product seven years ago and within two years was completely out of $100,000 worth of debt and had started a real estate portfolio—$35 at a time.

That's not to say you shouldn't focus on bigger things later, but first build up a series of small products or small successes—small victories if you will—to gain confidence and to pad your bank account.

Some of my favorite products and services that I have right now are $10, $17, and $27 dollars a month. You get enough of those going in different niches or different places—or even in the same market—and it adds up. It gives you room to breathe and it gives you room to create.

It serves your market and it also helps you build wealth and freedom at the same time. So, quit worrying about the million-dollar idea and focus on a million smaller ideas that can help you build wealth and maybe not freeze you with intimidation when you're worried about getting it perfect or competing with the "big boys" or "big girls," as it were.

I believe you can build freedom and wealth in modest amounts.

Part One

The Myth Breakers

One

Job Security, Tenure, Retirement, and Other Fairy Tales

You simply cannot spend your life in fear of losing your job, your health, your life or your wife. I decided that I had to create my own financial reality and job security. Was I afraid of failing? Yes, but I could continue being scared and broke, or I could be afraid and well paid. I chose the latter. At some point, you have to be more afraid of not trying than you are of failing.

—Carrie Wilkerson

Famous Last Words

"My husband has been working there so long, they will never lay him off."

"I'm invaluable to the team. My position is absolutely safe."

"My future is in my retirement funds. Those are secure."

"Our company is very stable. I don't have anything to worry about."

"Credit card debt is just normal; we're not in real financial trouble."

"I have a college degree. I won't have any trouble finding a great job."

Well, to quote Dr. Phil McGraw, "How's that working out for you?"

If you've picked up this book, you are interested in this topic. You either have a nagging feeling that your career isn't secure, your future is wobbly, or perhaps you've already been shaken to your core with unwelcome change and now you're just seeking answers. I don't need to wow you with statistics or convince you that added income and stability would be a good thing. You get that already.

Perhaps you have a great career but you're maxed out, stressed-out, and desperately want or need a transition. Great. This is for you too.

Okay, so hang with me for a little while and let's be honest. You may have been laid off. Your spouse maybe has been laid off, or your mom, your dad, your adult child, somebody in your neighborhood. Maybe your hours have been cut. Maybe you've been demoted or asked to take a pay cut. Maybe your core business has been slashed like one of my businesses has because of the recession. (Was that too honest? You'll find that about me. No sugarcoating.) One of my businesses that used to be my primary source of income is now at about 40 percent of the revenue it produced just three years ago—so I'm not immune to what we're talking about. As a matter of fact, that is why I'm so passionate about it. Because if I were still solely reliant on that one business, I'd be in trouble!

I'm here to give you some hope and to tell you how I recession-insulated myself before I even knew a recession was coming.

I am not a big proponent of the fear factor or panic-driven marketing. I don't want everybody running around like Chicken Little saying, "Oh, the sky is falling, the sky is falling, and it's all the president's fault." "It's all the last administration's fault." "Oh, if only the mortgage companies . . ." You know what, we can blame, blame, blame all we want and it's not going to help fix it.

I could blame my weight struggle on any number of factors if I wanted to be rid of the responsibility. The media has made it popular for me to blame genetics, fast-food places, additives in commercially prepared staples, and more. But the fact is, I have to own it and then I have to take the reins and go a different direction.

The recession is real and we're affected. Let's talk about what we can do about it. Okay? I hope you're nodding your head and you're with me.

Why do we need multiple streams of income? Why do we need "self-controlled and self-generated income"? Why? Well, for the primary reasons I told you about a minute ago, you don't want to be too reliant on a job. We all know that at the end of the day, the owner of the company is concerned about the owner of the company. Everybody else is expendable, period. That's true in my company.

At the end of the day, my husband and I are the only two who are guaranteed to have jobs on Friday—every Friday—from now till eternity in my company. That is just how it rolls. It doesn't make employers bad people. It doesn't make them selfish or uncaring. It's just economics; it's how it works.

The owner is in control of how the money is spent, and the owner is in control of who stays or who goes. So, you need to be the owner of a part-time or a full-time business.

Sounds almost too easy, doesn't it?

Kauffman Survey: "Nearly half of businesses started in the business owner's home or garage. Slightly more than 40% operated in rented or leased space, while the remaining operated at the site of a current client, or in a building or location bought by the business.

More than half of all businesses in the U.S. are run out of the home and employ more than venture-funded companies do. The reason for this growth is because of layoffs and a dull labor market."

—*Jerry Osteryoung, Director of Outreach at Florida State University's Jim Moran Institute for Global Entrepreneurship*

BAREFOOT ACTION STEP

Sounds Good, But She's . . .

Winners compare their achievements with their goals, while losers compare their achievements with those of other people.

—Nido Qubein

Watch the "Sounds Good, But She's . . ." video at http://barefootexecutivevideos.com/but

Today I want to talk a little bit about mind-set and something that, quite frankly, is tripping you up. We get caught in the "Yeah, but she's—" or the "Yeah, but he's—."

Well, sure she's doing great, but she's got a CFO, or she's got a team, or she has money to invest there, or she doesn't have kids at home, or her kids aren't in school, or she's married, or she's single, or she doesn't need to lose weight, or she's blah, blah, blah.

It's easy to look at the person on the other side of the camera or the other side of the bank account or the other side of the check or the other side of the table and make excuses for why you're not where he or she is. You need to quit comparing yourself to anyone else. Compare you to you. You be your best you. You are not going to do the same things as I am, or as he is, or as she is. You're not going to have the same family situation or the same life situation—maybe ever.

The truth is, all of us start at the same spot—zero. We all start with zero experience. Our life experience, our life stories, our work experience, our education, those add up to make us who we are. It's really easy to look at someone who is doing well and say, "That was easy for him because—." You are giving yourself permission not to push yourself. You *need* to push yourself. Turn your excuses into the reasons why you must succeed, the reasons why you must take action.

I've overcome more than one hundred pounds of extra weight, more than $100,000 of debt, several business failures, depression, and just obstacle after obstacle. I have four children and several businesses.

Yes, I have a team now. Yes, I have discretionary funding now. Yes, I seem as if I have it all together now. But the truth is, I've built step-by-step just as you're building step-by-step. So I'm qualified to say "Get over yourself, take action, quit comparing yourself to other people. That is suicide on the installment plan."

Just beat *your* best, do *your* best, and learn *your* best. Then take action, and you cannot help but be profitable and succeed on your terms.

BAREFOOT CASE STUDY

Paul B. Evans
Alabama
TeenLifeMinistries.com
Speaker, Author, Trainer
http://www.paulbevans.com
Personal Development

"Be who you are and work based on your strengths and not society's expectations."

My entire life has been built around ADD: bouncing from idea to idea and career to career before finding my place in the middle of chaos. Instead of a single focus, I tend to work on several projects at once to escape boredom and burnout.

For years I wondered if I was ever going to make it as "me." A good friend and I were talking one day and he talked about his life as an architect. He said he would have spurts of inspiration for a couple of weeks then collapse into mush for a week. He talked about the difference between a structured job and creative flexibility. For the first time I really "got" that it was fine to be who you are and to work based on your strengths and not society's expectations.

I've been married for seventeen years and now have two sons. My first wife and mother of one son died when he was five weeks old. After her death, my priorities realigned. One of the promises I made was that I would always be home for my family's events. I never wanted to tell them that I could not be there for them because of work. The only way for me to have that type of flexibility was to work on my own terms and set my own guidelines.

The title *personal development* sounds like a "motivational" market. You know, a bunch of guru types spouting "You can make it!" I'm definitely for a positive approach to life and believe in setting goals, but we need to be more realistic. Not everyone can change the world, but everyone can change *his own* world. Each person should recognize his strength and make it better in order to serve others, so others can become better and so on.

I also work to help orphans—it's amazing that so many innocents go without the basics. Even worse, that in many countries corrupt systems of government often abuse them. (As cofounder of 100xmissions.org, I give half my time to fund-raising there.)

A couple of times a month I think, *Have I lost my mind? I need a job with a predictable paycheck.* Of course, I then picture myself in a cubicle, chained to a desk, with the expectation of arriving and leaving at a certain time, and I come back to reality.

The truth is that being an entrepreneur is tough. It's stressful. Most folks act as if "working for yourself" is the ultimate vacation. But you're responsible for *everything*. While employees get paid for showing up and doing what they're told, entrepreneurs get paid for taking risks and even then income is not guaranteed.

I wish someone had said, "This is the hardest thing you'll ever do in your life. It will be worth it, but put away the magic beans."

Two

Why You Must Own a Business—and Fast

I have been impressed with the urgency of doing. Knowing is not enough; we must apply. Being willing is not enough; we must do.

—Leonardo da Vinci

First, I should tell you that reading this book might not be popular with your spouse, your parents, your friends, and most especially, your *boss*! Status quo is what is comfortable for those around you. The fact that you picked up this book automatically sets you apart. But that might not be a comfortable place for you.

We are surrounded by naysayers, by nonsupporters, by people who just don't understand, and you have to cut them a little slack. You do!

Number One

We are raised and reared to be job-minded, to be employee-minded. We are sent to school and then to high school and then to college, told to get a good job, work for somebody else, come home, turn on the TV, spend some time with our family, and then do it all again, Monday through Friday. (If you're lucky, you don't have to work weekends.)

That's how our society has been conditioned ever since the Industrial Revolution and the time of factories and unions and hours and set, standard working conditions. That is how our communities are trained, that's what is comfortable for people, that's what they know, and so that's what they're familiar with.

Whether this is your first business or your one-hundredth business, your community, the parents of the kids that your kids hang out with, the people in your church, your family, the people at reunions and holidays will not understand you and—let me go ahead and let you off the hook—*it is not your job to educate them all.*

You cannot make them understand. Some of them never will; and some of them simply are comfortable the way they are, and any growth or change in you makes them uncomfortable, so what's a body to do?

What you do is consciously choose whom you surround yourself with.

Social Media Surroundings

Self-selecting groups on Facebook, Twitter, and LinkedIn are an excellent way to surround yourself with like-minded people, achievers, and people who understand you. How so? Working at home can be lonely. The people in your neighborhood and your family have perhaps known you since your pre-expert days, and they won't necessarily give you the credibility you need or deserve. They also have likely seen you start a diet and quit, perhaps start an exercise program and quit. Maybe they've seen you quit a job or change career paths or focus on several different things, and they won't be the sound voices of encouragement or affirmation that you need.

Maybe your peers "in real life" are not goal focused and are trained as employees, so this entire "start a business" phenomenon is a little hard for them to grasp and get excited about. In social media, you choose who is in the sandbox with you. Want big thinkers? You can find them there. Want goal-oriented folks? They show up there too! Want to quickly find other business owners, folks in your business model, or even other people who follow the same "leaders" as you do? That's easier to do than ever by using social media, search tools, and self-selected groups.

Need encouragement? Go to these places and tap those folks. Want to see other folks achieving without being embarrassed about it? You can find them in social media for the same reason you're there. If nothing else, go to TwitterBarefoot.com or FacebookBarefoot.com and I'll cheer you on when you need it.

Live Events

Another way to find other like-minded people is through live events and workshops. Not necessarily just chamber events and networking events, where you're looking for clients and prospects or leads. Consider attending learning events for other business owners in your field, in your market, or even in new strategies for like-minded peers.

My annual event, "BE U," is a fabulous place to meet kindred spirits who are driven by their dreams. Every year in October, I bring in hundreds of small business owners to Dallas, Texas, for encouragement, education, and even some entertainment. We've featured famous speakers, such as Zig Ziglar and Dr. John C. Maxwell, but mostly speakers who are ordinary folks doing extraordinary things in business. I only invite speakers I've learned from, those I trust, and those with an extreme sense of integrity.

This is a "non-salesy" event, meaning the speakers aren't selling from the stage, they are teaching from the heart and they are attentive and interactive with the attendees during breaks, lunch, and sessions. In addition, we have breakout sessions during lunch, power networking. I really enjoy this "Barefoot family reunion" every year. What a thrill and honor to be in the presence of people with goals, visions, and dreams for their lives and their families.

For more information and to get on our notification list, you can go to BarefootExecutive.TV and click on the button with the BE U pennant. We don't want you to miss out if this sounds like your kind of crowd.

Masterminds and Mentors

I often seek out folks to support me intentionally, because sometimes the people around me don't understand. They don't understand:

- my ambition
- what I'm doing with my business model
- that my husband works at home with me

- why we're home and around town during the day
- why I travel for business when I don't have a job
- why I can't always drop everything to go play (After all, I'm home and should be able to go have coffee with them when they call.)
- that it's not about the money

Does any of that sound familiar?

I tend to have a very different social circle—a very intentional social circle. I pay to be part of a "mastermind." (We'll talk more about this in chapters 8 and 9.) I pay to be part of business groups and I purposely attend high-caliber events where I can be with people who are achievers, big thinkers, big action takers, and in a business model similar to mine.

That's how I feed my business mind, that's how I stay sharp. The Bible says that iron sharpens iron, so I choose to surround myself with sharp people, and by doing that, sometimes "paying to play"—call it whatever you want—I have discovered a handful of people who are my lifelong kindred spirits and best friends, and we do life together.

I didn't discover them in my town. I didn't just happen upon them. I found them intentionally. Are you hearing that? I intentionally surround myself with sharp people.

Recently I spent a few days in New York with some of my top partners from a promotion. Through some of my contacts and networks, we spent some time with businessman, author, and social media expert Gary Vaynerchuk from Wine Library TV. We visited Gary's studios and I introduced my promotion partners to him and to some other influencers in the marketing arena.

These are people whom I had chosen to spend three days with. I chose to introduce them to other people in my network, in this case, a high-powered speaker and author, Gary "Vee." Suzanne Evans, one of the participants, said, "I got into the space of Carrie Wilkerson on purpose because Carrie has surrounded herself with the most amazing high-caliber, quality people. I cannot even imagine the people that I'm sitting at this table with." (We were at a sandwich shop with four other authors, speakers, and international business builders. It was very cool.)

When you surround yourself with people of high caliber, then you begin to draw other people of high caliber. There is a powerful magnetic effect.

There is a really strong, high caliber of people at BE U because they know that I surround myself intentionally and that they will meet some amazing people. It challenges them to be their very best too.

BE U is short for "Barefoot Executive University" and the entire theme is "Be Exceptional. Be Extraordinary. Be You."

Leave Your House

I initially began my work teaching and speaking as the Barefoot Executive primarily because working at home felt so alone and different from what everyone else was doing. How do you combat isolation, insecurity, and other obstacles that we all encounter? I believe you should embrace social networking, live events, local networking groups, your local or greater area chamber meetings, Tweetups, and a mastermind or inner circle. Just trust me when I say, if you are depending on family reunions, PTA meetings, and church to satisfy your need for meaningful social interaction with other businesses, you are sorely mistaken. It just won't be enough and you'll find yourself "stuck."

Find a Forum

Be part of a targeted forum or two. I remember when I started my investigation into the world of growing my business online, my whole purpose was to connect the work-at-home community because I had been feeling alone, isolated, insecure, uncertain, and as if I were the only one doing what I was doing. So I wanted to form a community online to attract and surround myself with other people working at home. I joined a forum for membership site owners, operated by a friend of mine.

On that forum I started talking to people about what they were doing, what their new Web sites were going to be, and what their interests were. I got involved in several conversations. As a result, several people I met became very strong allies, and we have likely added multiple six figures to each other's incomes through cross-promotions, cocreated products, and introductions to each other's connections.

Don't underestimate the power of a forum but do choose your forums wisely. You typically get what you pay for. A free forum has other people looking for free forums, so that's all I'll say about that. A forum can be a very powerful way to connect, especially if your time is limited, your travel is limited, and you are a little nervous. So connect with some people on forums. Be careful of the negative forums and "bash and trash" forums. The folks hanging out there are not being profitable or productive in their businesses or lives. Be as selective about whom you spend time with online as you are in person.

Get a Coach

Perhaps the best way to combat isolation and the Lone Ranger syndrome is to hire a powerful coach who is where you want to be, who has achieved a measure of success, who has encountered some of the same obstacles as you, and who is not afraid to be honest and blunt with you. You need to find a coach or mentor, or a consultant. That is the number one way to find somebody like-minded and to be accountable.

The other benefit is that you are one degree away from everybody they know. That is a powerful way to build alliances and a strong network and to combat some isolation.

The truth is, nobody totally "gets" you, nobody totally "gets" me—they don't totally understand us—and guess what? That is okay!

What Will "Qualify" You?

After I had been in business for about five years, I had become really profitable, had climbed out of a lot of debt, and had great nationwide influence in one of my businesses. I was doing really well—high profit margins, lean business machine. Loved it.

But it started bugging me that I didn't have a business degree. I have a mass communications degree, and I felt that in order to be an authentic businessperson I should have an MBA. So I started researching MBA programs and looking around and even filled out the paperwork to apply for a program several semesters in a row. For whatever reason, I kept putting it off. And finally my husband, who does have an MBA, asked me, "Carrie, why do you want an MBA?"

"Well, I think it will make me a better businessperson. I think it'll make me more qualified."

"Are you going to get a promotion in your own company when you have an MBA?"

"Well, no."

"Will you get a raise? Will your clients say, 'We want to pay you more because now you have an MBA'?"

"Well, no."

"Do your clients look on your Web site to see if you have an MBA before they do business with you?"

"Hmm, no."

He said, "Then why don't you invest that money and that time into learning skills, studying with mentors, being in a mastermind, doing things that directly impact your bottom line? The only way another degree directly impacts your bottom line is if you work for someone else and it's a requirement; otherwise, it takes away from your bottom line because of how much it costs you."

(He was, of course, completely right. But please don't tell him I said that.) I'm a fan of higher learning. I totally hope my kids go to college. I'm planning for that, we talk about it with the kids, and we have funded it in anticipation of their decisions. I think college is necessary for a lot of young people to learn about paying their dues. And of course if you're in a field like medicine or law or teaching, there are reasons that you go to school.

But as far as an established businessperson going back to school to say, "Yes, now I'm qualified to do business," it didn't make a lot of sense for me.

Before you rush into another certification program or investigate degrees in order to run your business, ask those same questions my husband asked me and see if you are just using the credentials as a way to validate yourself.

BAREFOOT ACTION STEP

Be a Solution Finder, Not a Victim

The greatest challenge to any thinker is stating the problem in a way that will allow a solution.

—**Bertrand Russell**

Watch the "Be a Solution Finder, Not a Victim" video at http://barefootexecutivevideos.com/solution

Today has been one of those days.

When you have an online business or a business with an online component, you have to wrestle what I call "technical alligators." That means sometimes your Internet is not working right, sometimes you get hacked, sometimes you have viruses, sometimes things just aren't flowing the way they need to.

Part of this is my fault, but I had coaching calls today with my inner circle clients, I had a webinar mid-afternoon using streaming video, and several other things going on. My Internet went down and then it was just one thing right after another.

I already had a technical person handling my webinar with my guest expert, so that was okay, except that my audience paid for me to introduce it and usually I facilitate the Q&A. I could have been frustrated, I could have freaked out, but instead I chose what I've adopted as a solution-oriented mind-set.

I like to think outside the box: *How can I make this work? How can I stay calm? How can I not give negative energy to this today*? I can't control the Internet company, I don't want to change the webinar schedule, people have paid to be part of that series and they've paid handsomely, and my guest has set aside his day to teach for me.

So, I used my telephone to record an introduction on Audio Acrobat, I called my technical guy and gave him access to download the introduction from my Audio Acrobat panel, and I recorded an outro—or the ending, the wrap-up of the call.

I explained what was going on with my Internet, I graciously introduced my guest just as as I would have if I'd been on the call, and my technical person uploaded all of it for the beginning and the end. Problem solved.

I wasn't there, but it showed my audience how to handle a challenge with grace, it handled the problem, and I didn't have to change the schedule. I didn't have to be mad at the Internet company, because I was able to be a little bit flexible. In the meantime I'd been taking coaching calls, too, and working with some of my high-level clients.

I was still smiling. I was a little frazzled, it took a lot of energy, but I handled it. My business was still running, I wasn't mad at anybody—I'm a little frustrated with my Internet, but I'll get that resolved.

I used solution-focused thinking instead of victim thinking or instead of a frazzled, *What am I going to do now*? kind of thinking. Nobody gets anything accomplished by freaking out. I guess I learned that from my dad, who was in the Coast Guard for twenty-seven years in search and rescue.

He taught me: "Carrie, you handle a situation, you handle the rescue, you can fall apart emotionally later. Just get the job done right now." That advice has served me well with my four children—with various bumps, bruises, scrapes, and emergency room visits. It has served me well in some relationship catastrophes and has served me well in business.

How can you be solution focused? How can you be the "search and rescue" for your business? What can you handle now and have it come apart later when it doesn't matter so much?

Being reactive and being a victim don't serve anyone, most especially you.

17

BAREFOOT CASE STUDY

Jim Palmer
Chester County, Pennsylvania
www.NewsletterGuru.TV
Client Retention Specialist

"Focus on serving your customers with world-class service and place a higher emphasis on client retention instead of client acquisition."

The entrepreneurial bug first bit me early in my life, and after only two years of college I left to become a store manager. My dreams of becoming the ultimate retailer and businessman were immediately and seriously challenged because this was during the severe recession of the early 1980s. I was deeply concerned because the business I was now in charge of was literally shrinking before my eyes with fewer and fewer customers coming into the bike shop every day. Money was so tight that we'd turn out the lights to save electricity when no customers were in the store, and we'd then quickly turn them on if we heard a car door in the parking lot.

To add to my stress as a businessman, I was newly married and my wife was pregnant with our first child. My biggest fear was that the business would close, I would lose my job, and effectively "crash and burn" on my first time at bat. Fear is a great motivator, so I got to work and developed a marketing and business-building strategy to grow the bike shop into one of the largest volume stores in the country.

We couldn't afford more traditional forms of marketing, such as radio, newspaper, and TV, so I sat down at a typewriter and wrote my first newsletter. We distributed the newsletter to everyone on our customer list and to a strategic list of prospective customers. To my pleasant surprise to our small two-page, black-and-white newsletter started bringing in new business almost immediately, so I did what any smart marketer would do, I wrote and mailed more newsletters!

Thanks in large part to the success of our newsletter, we developed stronger and more profitable relationships with our customers and we were able to grow that bike shop from $330K in sales to $960K in fewer than four years. At the time, the average bike shop in the United States was grossing approximately $250K.

After ten years as manager, I was recruited to be a regional manager for a competitor. We later franchised this business, and I was promoted to director of franchise operations. My career and income were progressing nicely, and I was proud that my wife could be a stay-at-home mom for our four children all these years. But, as I look back today, I realize that my life was out of balance and my priorities were not what they should have been. I was focusing too much on acquiring things and not enough on giving back and serving others.

That all changed in a major way when I suddenly lost my job as vice president of sales and marketing for a training company. To make matters even more stressful, if that was possible, while still unemployed I was diagnosed with melanoma. Recuperating from my surgery, while I was truly grateful to be alive and hopefully cancer free, my all-consuming thought was what I was going to do next. It was then that I began to pray for guidance and wisdom. It became apparent to me that I was to start my own business.

Since starting my first business in November 2001, I've achieved substantial growth by practicing and applying the same marketing and business-building strategies I developed back in 1982 to save the bike shop from bankruptcy: focus on serving your customers with world-class service and place a higher emphasis on client retention instead of client acquisition (maximizing the profit potential of every customer).

When I started my business, I knew instantly that newsletters would be my main offering; today I'm known internationally as the Newsletter Guru. I have the pleasure of serving hundreds of clients in nine countries through No Hassle Newsletters, No Hassle Social Media, and the Newsletter Guru's Concierge Print and Mail on Demand Service. I also coach other entrepreneurs on developing smart, effective strategies for maximizing the profitability of their customer relationships.

My priorities have shifted from building a life full of acquiring things to focusing on how I can use my success to make a difference in the lives of others. My two biggest passions are feeding the homeless and rehabbing homes for low-income people. Our mission is to make the homes we work on warmer, safer, and drier.

I love my business because it's fun and affords me the opportunity to help other entrepreneurs and make a positive difference in their businesses and, therefore, hopefully in their lives. There's nothing more energizing or exciting than creating and building a business. My kids are grown now, but when I started my business they were home and I got to see them much more than when I worked for someone else.

How hard was I tested? My entire first year of business was revenue free. That's a nice way of saying that it took me twelve months to get my first client! As I continued to rack up debt, I also knew that God appreciates and rewards hard work, so I got a job stocking shelves. I worked the 5:00 a.m. shift until noon and then went home to make sales calls. At night I went to networking events and then home to bed to get up at 4:00 the next morning. I did this for more than a year until my business growth required me to quit. Tested, yes; scared beyond belief, you bet; but I never wanted to quit.

What have I learned?

1. To recognize the value of investing in myself. I am a huge reader, but beyond books, I think I'm talking about coaches, mentors, and mastermind groups. The expense always seemed to precede the income so it was a leap of faith for all of them, but one that always paid off.
2. To shed my "must be perfect" corporate way of doing things and learn the value of massive action and the power of thinking big.
3. To trust the power of tithing and giving back. I wish I had learned and trusted the power of tithing and giving back sooner. It's quite scary when you don't have money, but I have learned these last few years that you can't outgive God.

PART ONE RECAP

Let's just highlight, shall we? Tooth Fairy, Santa Claus, Easter Bunny, and Job Security all fall into the same category. They just don't exist. They're fun to think about and easy to believe in, but when the truth finally comes out—and it always does—there is a sinking feeling and a wondering why "no one told me this before."

Building a business will require a rebel attitude and a maverick-type resolve. This is against the status quo, it's not easy, and not everyone will be supportive of your efforts. That's okay because you can get some "peer insurance" for those tough times.

Peer insurance? Surround yourself with like-minded and goal-oriented individuals, using one or more of these methods:

- *Networking groups* like BNI and your local chamber of commerce
- *Social networking sites* like Twitter, Facebook, and LinkedIn
- *Live business events* like BE U—the event I host annually in Dallas in October
- *Online forums* (choose wisely and don't overdo)
- *Plug into my sites* (BarefootExecutive.TV is a great start)
- *Hire the support* of a coach or mentor

And finally, quit believing that you have to "credentialize" yourself or qualify yourself before you are able to successfully run your business. You already have great experience, skills, and an opportunity to serve. Don't wait for someone to give you permission. Consider it granted!

Part Two

The Three Big Mistakes

Three

Mistake Number 1: Chasing Someone Else's Dream

We must look for ways to be an active force in our own lives. We must take charge of our own destinies, design a life of substance and truly begin to live our dreams.

—Les Brown

One common mistake that people make, that business owners make, is pursuing things that are totally unrelated to what they're doing now—something foreign to them, something with a 100 percent new learning curve, something someone else believes is a good fit or that they've seen someone else doing. We've all known someone who was learning the family business by "default" because that is what was expected of them. They might have zero interest in the market or service, but it is their parents' dream.

What about seeing other people excelling and deciding that is the field you need to be in because they love it so much and are doing so well? We tend to think, *Oh, I could do that too!* But that is *their* dream, not necessarily what is the best fit for you.

When I first started implementing streams of income (see chapters 14–16), the most common one I heard about was real estate. I owned a home and had owned a few other homes previously, but I had not done investment real estate. So I thought, *Okay, that's what I hear people talking about. I'm going to invest in real estate. That's how I'm going to diversify.*

I jumped in with both feet, as is my habit. Some of you are laughing and nodding because that's your habit too. I made a lot of mistakes and they were expensive.

I still have some of those properties and I've corrected some of my mistakes. But I didn't have experience in real estate. I was not currently functioning in real estate. I didn't spend a lot of time studying real estate. I didn't have any business trying to make that a multiple stream of income before I was ready.

I now have a client who is well versed in real estate investing and has an extreme passion for it. It is his dream. It is what he knows and what he does really well. But it's okay for that to be his dream and not to be mine. I need to get comfortable pursuing my own dream, with my own skills, and on my own terms.

Instead of pursuing real estate first thing, I should have focused on what I was doing and diverted my experience. I should have diverted the water stream instead of trying to dig a trench where none had existed before. I hope that word picture helped you. You don't need to dig a trench where none has existed before. Let's look at your current source and let's see how we can branch off some other streams from that. Otherwise you're going to waste a lot of time and money trying to figure out something that likely isn't a good fit for you. And it *surely* isn't going to be the quickest way to extra income or security.

Instead, let's consider a dentist who has built a thriving practice. Dr. David Phelps is branching out his streams of income by teaching practice growth techniques to other dental experts. Because of a medical condition that his daughter battles, he also has developed systems and strategies to get himself out of the office and more involved in her life and is teaching other dentists how to remove themselves from the daily grind of their practice, while still having a thriving business, full appointment book, and growing bank account. His streams of income are related to his expertise and his direct skill sets. As a result, his practice came to a level of profitability more quickly than if he'd started something random, unrelated, and new.

BAREFOOT ACTION STEP

You Have to Suit Up and Show Up

It was character that got us out of bed, commitment that moved us into action, and discipline that enabled us to follow through.

—**Zig Ziglar**

Watch the "You Have to Suit Up & Show Up" video at http://barefootexecutivevideos.com/suitup

Today I'm dressed to work out. Since I've lost a lot of weight, it's been a constant struggle for me to keep it off. It's something that I have to consciously keep an eye on—what I'm eating and how I'm moving and all those things. My fitness expert friends swear that at some point I'm going to enjoy working out and I'll look forward to it because of the high I get, but I guess I'm not quite there yet because I still have to force myself to do it.

I still have to make time in my day for it; I still have to convince myself that it's better for me than not. It's not always easy, but I do find that it's easier when I'm consistent, scheduled, and doing the kind of things that my body responds to positively—like a routine. Then I have results.

When I stop doing what I'm supposed to be doing, when I don't schedule it—I get busy and schedule over it or just never get around to it—then I don't work out the way I should or how I respond best. It occurs to me that your business is very much that same way. Right?

We have to "suit up," we have to schedule work on our business, and we have to do the correct activities. We have to do what the trainer prescribes for us—our coach or our mentor—or even our associates if we're working on joint ventures and affiliates and those kinds of things.

It's not always fun each and every day, but when you put your time in, when you have consistent activity, then you're guaranteed results. They may not come as fast as you want them to, they may not be as big as you want them to be, but you will have results.

And you'll be encouraged by those results, whether it's in business or in fitness, so you suit up and you do it again. In fitness you can lose progress when you sit back and relax and don't dress out and don't get to the equipment or don't get to your routine—and business works the same way.

I encourage you to do five things a day. Jack Canfield calls it the "Five a Day Rule" and John C. Maxwell calls it the "Law of Five." And I'm a believer. Five things a day—five activities on your business today.

Five auto-responders, five note cards, five follow-ups, five phone calls, five written articles, five pages of your book, shoot five videos, brainstorm and outline five ideas, five pages that you read, five product development thoughts, five PowerPoint slides, five pictures that you post, five new contacts or conversations on social media, five something!

If you consistently discipline yourself for those five things a day, then it usually turns into six, seven, eight, nine, and ten. When the results start pouring in, maybe you'll aim for six things a day or seven things a day.

I am encouraged to work out because I see results physically—I feel results in my health, I have better energy, my metabolism is better—and I know that will improve the quality of my life. The same is true in my business.

I suit up, I make myself put in the time, put in the five a day. Some days it's only five and some days it's many more than five, but I've seen the results. I'm empowered, I'm impassioned, and I'm encouraged by those results, and I want you to be too.

BAREFOOT CASE STUDY 1

Marcia Hawkins
Utah
Digital Scrapbooking

**"I'm a people person. I absolutely love meeting
new 'friends' through my business."**

I was diagnosed with multiple sclerosis in 1998. Shortly after, I found out I was pregnant with my youngest child. Although I enjoyed my job immensely, it was stressful and my health started to deteriorate. So, after lots of long hours of talks with my husband and many prayers, I decided that it was best for me to quit my job and take care of my health. After all, if I didn't take care of myself, who would take care of my family?

I knew that after working for twenty-plus years, I was going to go crazy at home all day without doing something to keep me busy. I have always loved scrapbooking and got interested in digital scrapbooking about the same time that I quit my job. So, I posted an ad on eBay for digital scrapbooking. I get just enough business to keep me busy, but not overwhelmed. It gives me a little extra cash to help out with replacing the income that I had before. It also is fun to meet new people through what I love to do.

I'm a people person. I absolutely love meeting new "friends" through my business. It's fun to get to know their stories and watch their families grow. For example, I met Carrie on eBay when her third child was born and have now been scrapbooking for her for about seven years.

Because I work from home, I can set my own hours, my own rates, and choose who my clients are.

BAREFOOT CASE STUDY 2

Pam Garner Moore
Louisiana
www.marykay.com/pgarnermoore
Direct Sales

"I should swim in my own lane and not compare myself to anyone."

I was a nerdy, shy college kid when direct sales found me. A totally unlikely candidate who wore no makeup, could not say my name out loud in front of any group, large or small, and with no confidence at all in anything but my values and my academic ability. I began dabbling in my new entrepreneurial world, never dreaming it would become my profession. What I found, though, in addition to a way to make a life and a living, was a cure for the painful shyness that plagued me. For an hour or two with a client, I was forced to forget about myself and think, instead, about that client.

Upon finishing college, I chose to make this very part-time venture my full-time vocation. And so I have had the blessing of being self-employed since college—a journey that has given me way more than I could have guessed or prayed for or expected, both tangible and intangible.

I started my business with only a mild curiosity and the thought that if it were what it appeared to be, it would be perfect. I did not think that it would work, that I would be good at it, nor that I would like it. I determined to give it a year of honest effort and to quit when I proved all of the above to be correct assumptions. That was thirty-one years ago.

I love serving women. I think that women are *amazing* creatures who do so much so well but often in the process forget to take care of themselves. I simply could not *not* do what I do. It is who I am, what I am called to do, and I could not work for free, but I love it so much that I would.

I wish I'd known when I started that I already had what I needed inside to do this and do it well—that I just had to step into that place. It took learning to swim in my own lane and not comparing myself to anyone.

Four

Mistake Number 2:
Chasing Too Many Rabbits

Those who are blessed with the most talent don't necessarily outperform everyone else. It's the people with follow-through who excel.

—**Mary Kay Ash**

A big mistake I see people make is that they choose to jump all over the place with their revenue streams. They're going to invest in real estate and the stock market and gold, they're going to do an online business, they're going to have a flower shop, and then—(you get the idea, right?). I won't make virtual eye contact here in case this refers to you specifically. And let me be clear that I'm not beating anyone over the head here; I am speaking from direct experience of my own. I have experienced the same phenomenon with hundreds of thousands of comments, responses, questions, and hundreds of personal clients.

What happens is they may have a little success in all those areas, but they're going to have a hard time getting massive success in any area unless they focus on one area until they get it to what I call "ridiculous cash." It gets pleasantly profitable when you can breathe, when you feel comfortable enough with that system. You can then either replicate it or apply it to another area.

If you have a job right now, then focus on a part-time area somewhat related to your skill set, your software, your space, and the experience you have to offer. But don't try to say, "Oh, I'm going to do real estate, and I'm going to do this, and I'm going to start a Web site" all at the same time.

Mary Kay Ash, whom I consider my mentor even though we never met personally, said, "You cannot chase two rabbits at the same time and catch either one." That's true. But you can chase one rabbit, catch him, and get the system down. Then you can either put systems in place to outsource chasing the second rabbit or, once you've got the first one tied up, go chase the other one yourself.

It's not that you can't have multiple streams of income. But you can't be in the building phase with all of them at the same time. You can't pursue more than one new thing at the same time. You have to be able to focus on one to "ridiculous cash" and then focus on the others. Then, guess what?

- You're profitable enough to breathe, which helps free your creative mind.
- This frees your bank account for some investment in education, like a home-study course, a mentor, or a mastermind group.
- You figure out which systems work for you—that you are comfortable with—and then you can duplicate those in other areas, thus making your next streams more profitable, more quickly.

We've all been there with the "Oh, I'm stressed-out and my shoulders are permanently up to my ears." Your first stream of income or your job allows you to relax a little. You cannot function with the big *D* of desperation on your head; it's just too stifling to work that way. Sometimes the best advice I can give a struggling start-up client is, "Get a part-time or full-time job first—then start working on your business." It seems counterintuitive, I know—but it's just how the laws of time management, energy management, and desperation sometimes work.

You say, "Oh, but Carrie, I am desperate right now. I'm here because:

- I've been pink-slipped."
- my retirement account has tanked."
- my wife has had a baby and wants to stay home."
- my child has become ill and we need the extra income."

You still need to focus on one initial stream. When you get it to a comfortable level of cash, then you can add your second stream. I know you might be frustrated with that advice, but I promise you, it really does work best.

BAREFOOT ACTION STEP

Don't Hold Back—Give It Away

I have found that the more I seek to offer solutions for my marketplace, the more I grow in return. I heard Andy Horner, founder of Premier Designs, say, "Stop selling and start serving." That's just simple genius.

—Carrie Wilkerson

Watch the "Don't Hold Back—Give It Away" video at http://barefootexecutivevideos.com/giveaway

I'll be the first to tell you that you need to value what you do and what you bring to the community and the expertise that you offer, and that you are worth charging for. Yes, yes, and yes. You know I believe that; it's in almost every course I teach.

I'm also a list builder, a lead generator, and a prospect seeker, however, and I believe the way that Baskin Robbins and grocery stores and so many businesspeople get you to fall in love with their product and become comfortable with them to the point of purchase is through sampling, through free content.

Baskin Robbins does not keep a special carton of substandard ice cream under the counter for sample tasters—they serve you the premium stuff. Because why? Because they want you to buy, they want you to trust them, and they want you to like what you taste.

When I offer free things in exchange for a name and an e-mail address—free articles, free audios, reports, e-books, or whatever it is that I choose in my business; maybe it's samples, consultations, strategy sessions, or treatments—why would I offer less than my best?

The truth of the matter is we get a little scarcity minded and we say, "If I give them my best then they won't need what I'm selling; they won't have any need to give me their money." The truth is, if you give them your best, they learn to know you, to like you, to trust you, and then to pay you.

When I teach a free class, do a webinar and open it to the public, write an article, do a podcast, or shoot my TV episodes, I pour my guts out. I don't hold anything back. You may think that's not wise, but I have seven figures a year that say differently.

I mean it. Don't hold back. It makes your audience not trust you. Teach them—teach them what they want to know. Don't hold secrets; don't keep the veil on. Don't say, "Oh and if you buy, then I'll show you the real stuff." What kind of trust is that building?

I know that's a popular tactic. But it's not my style. I believe if you teach and teach for free, then they'll pay you to teach and teach some more. It can only bless you and it can only bless them.

Yes, some people will take advantage. Yes, some people will sample your stuff and can figure it out from there. Great! Look at the people you've served—awesome. Has that taken anything away from you? Has your business gone backward because of that? I don't think so.

This past year I had an idea for a webinar. I put up the registration page and the video and offered it as a free webinar. Initially I wanted to charge for it, but then I got so excited about the topic, I got so excited about teaching an audience again, that I decided to open it up to the public and do it for free.

The reason I'm passionate about this is because in the first hour and fifteen minutes we had 469 people say, "Yes, I'm interested in that topic. Yes, I want to learn from you."

We eventually had almost two thousand people register for the free class, and at the end I said, "If you found value in this, the PayPal button on this page goes to my favorite charity, and you could change some lives with a donation of any amount. Please, go there and make a donation of what you felt the value of this webinar was to you." That was a win-win-win.

It didn't take anything away from me but an hour of my time, and it blessed my charity beyond belief.

What if five or ten people had hope again or got an aha! moment or changed their skill sets? What if it affects a mom so that she can affect her child's life? What if the information changes somebody's family the way this topic has changed my family? What if somebody is as blessed as I've been blessed? Why would I begrudge that? Why would I hold that back?

I challenge you today to give away some of your best stuff, to create some amazing stuff. Create something free that you're excited about teaching or sharing or giving. Yes, we need to monetize our businesses, but I believe the best intake method is often the "sample spoonful." It doesn't work *just* for ice cream.

BAREFOOT CASE STUDY

Leanne Ely
Charlotte, North Carolina
SavingDinner.com
Menu Planning

"Surround yourself with talented people, give them a lot of room to show you what they can do, then be generous with them to keep them!"

I had my own catering company in my early twenties and was successful early on, beating out many older, more established catering companies for a huge catering contract. This basically accelerated my love of food, cooking, serving, presentation, the whole bit. I learned as I went along and had some help from great chefs along the way. You could say I had a lot of chutzpah to think so big so early in life, but I have always been like that. My parents told me I could be anything I wanted to be and I believed them.

Since I always wanted to write, I self-published a little cookbook that was later picked up by a small label. I started the original menu-planning site online, the namesake of my cookbook, SavingDinner.com, and it took off like gangbusters. I had a literary agent within a year after that, and my first "real" book went to auction, with sixteen major houses bidding on it. Five years later, I have nine books under my belt, one of which became a *New York Times* best seller (for eight weeks!), helping me meet my goal (since middle school) of being on that coveted list.

I grew up in the '70s with a standard-issue home: two working parents, two siblings, a dog, and dinner every night at the dinner table. My mom was a good family cook with a great meat loaf, fabulous mashed potatoes, and a roast beef dinner every Sunday. My British father, on the other hand, was a wild gourmet cook, teaching me to eat garlicky frog legs at six years old and making all kinds of exotic ethnic cuisine that required a trip to an ethnic market and, come cooking time, a fire extinguisher and prayer the kitchen wouldn't blow up. Not all creations were successes, but many of them were. It made for an interesting home life for sure!

I saw a need: too many families floundering without that cornerstone of the family meal. It was disappearing. I investigated further and dis-covered an appalling lack of skill in the next generation—they couldn't cook or meal plan and thought the kitchen was the place that the large appliances were stored. I felt it my mission to don my cape and save their dinners by teaching them how to cook, meal plan, and get their culinary acts together. That's what I did, and it's what I do—passionately, for more than ten years now.

The people I serve want my help and I love helping them. I love their stories, their successes, and their loyalty. I understand why doctors feel such satisfaction in helping their patients. I feel that same satisfaction when I help them "operate" on their kitchens, meal plans, and family dinners. It's immensely satisfying.

As long as they will have me, I'm at their service.

I start in the morning with coffee and e-mail. Then I work through my planner and all the things I need to knock out for the day. My staff is geographically all over the place—we use Skype to conduct business virtually and I love it. There are blog posts to be written, menus to approve, and brainstorming sessions with my staff as well as new business ideas to be discussed. It's way more than full time, but I love every second of it.

We were the first menu-planning site online. We keep changing and evolving as our market dictates, plus we teach—we don't just throw product at our readers. Our Web site is all about empowering our audience and getting them out of that "I don't know how" place.

I remember standing out on my screen porch crying and telling a friend, "I can't do it anymore, I'm through, I'm not making enough money to keep this up." She told me to stop it, get a grip, and look at what I *did* have. She encouraged me to do the next thing. So I did and I've never looked back.

You need to have the right people working for you. If you don't, your business cannot grow. Surround yourself with talented people, give them a lot of room to show you what they can do, and then be generous with them to keep them!

Five

Mistake Number 3: Chasing Dollars

People are like large mouth bass, they like anything that is shiny.

—Dave Ramsey

Pursuing something just for the trendiness of it or the "market-hotness" of it will not build a business for you. (Yes, as a business owner you can make up your own words too.) You sometimes hear about "ground floor" opportunities.

"Jump on this before there is market saturation."
"We're sitting on a gold mine."
"This is where all the money is right now."
"If you really want a profitable market, go after _____."

This is not to say that none of this will ever apply to your personal market or skill set. Pursuing opportunity just for the sake of opportunity, however, is rarely a satisfying or profitable venture, in my opinion.

There is an entire market of "opportunity-seekers"—and that's not really the market I work with. My clients are business builders, sustainability seekers, and legacy casters. The biggest mistake I see is when individuals jump after the "shiny" stuff, as Dave Ramsey mentions at the opening of this chapter.

There is a time and a place for saying, "I need to embrace this trend in the industry and teach it or use it in my business." Social media is something that's hot right now. I have embraced it as a tool in my business. I have not embraced it as a business model. I have not embraced it as if I'm going to be the next social media speaker on every stage.

I'm not pursuing social media as my stream of income. I can add it to my toolbox of promotional tools for my business, however, without chasing it as a "new" thing to replace my business. Does that difference make sense to you?

Don't pursue something just because it's hot. I call that the "bright shiny objects" syndrome. Opportunity chasers think, *Oh, this is the solution here;* and then, *Oh no, this is the solution here;* and yet again, *This is the solution here.* You need to pursue something because it's related to your initial stream or your core business. Pursue it because you can have some sustainability, some credibility, and some flexibility within that model.

When you spend thousands of dollars on these "fixes," these "solutions," these "moneymakers," these "tests"—whatever is the newest and shiniest business model—it is not going to be good.

I'm sorry, but the opportunistic method is killing me. It's killing my customers. It's distracting and it's disheartening. Some of you feel that you can't make it in business because you've tried so many things and "nothing is working." The truth is, you haven't tried anything with a whole heart, a whole purpose, and your whole focus to cash. You've been chasing all the little dreams.

We can relate that very easily to the weight-loss market. I've struggled with a weight problem since my preteen years, and I've been on every diet known to humankind. I've spent thousands of dollars on supplements, books, treatments, and special foods. I've started over on almost every Monday of my life. However, you will never hear me say, "That diet doesn't work." The truth is—I believe every diet probably works. It's a matter of focusing on one, sticking with that diet, eating less than your body requires, drinking more water, moving your body, and focusing for a set period of time.

Your business is the same way. Stop looking for miracles; lace up your tennis shoes and get to walking! Walk in the rain, in the cold, in the heat. Walk when you're tired, when you're bored, when you're hungry. Walk when your feelings are hurt, when you have a headache, and when the scale doesn't seem to be moving. Focus on the right activities consistently and, in your diet as well as in your business, you will see improvement.

Yes, you will see advertisements, marketing messages, and articles about the "new and improved" methods and models for diets and business. But those are based on the fact that many marketers know you want the easy solution—the shiny object—and you want permission to give up easily on the hard work.

Ouch. I know that won't be popular. But the fact is, my jeans fit the way that they do because of the food and exercise choices I make, not because diets don't work or one workout machine is better than another.

Your bank account looks the way that it does because of the choices you are making.

Maybe you have been trying whatever looks easy, whatever looks hot, and whatever looks great. Stop it! I'm going to tell you, stop it—stop spending on every solution, every turnkey, every Easy button, and every bright shiny object. There is no Easy button. Business can be simple, but it's not easy. It requires work. It requires a proven method and, in some cases, the accountability of a mentor who is where you want to be.

So, you are not a work-oriented person; you are afraid to put in effort to make a stream of income work for you. If you're expecting me to say, "Buy this software and it's going to add a thousand dollars a month to what you're doing," then you probably should stop reading. I am "lucky" in business because I am focused and persistent.

Most miss opportunity because it shows up
in overalls and looks a lot like work.

—Ben Franklin

I'm talking about functioning with your core influence, your core integrity, and your core purpose. It's the gift that you were blessed to serve with in order to bless yourself and your family with the gifts of cash, choices, and options. I feel very strongly about it, in case you can't tell.

BAREFOOT ACTION STEP

What Fuels You

To live an extraordinary life, you must *resist the ordinary.*
—**Frank McKinney**

**Watch the "What Fuels You" video
at http://www.barefootexecutivevideos.com/ordinary**

Today I came into my office before everybody got up and I found a card on my desk, propped up on my keyboard. I wrapped up a really big project yesterday, something that I've been excited about. When I say really big, it wasn't a huge launch, it wasn't a huge landmark product, but it was something that I replicated that has been creating fifteen hundred to twenty-one hundred dollars a month in revenue, almost passively (which is fun).

I also created a similar product yesterday in a different target market. My husband knew I had been working really hard on it and that I was really excited about it. Before bed I showed him all the Web pages, the lead-in pages, the marketing materials, and the whole process. And we were really excited and proud.

Well, I woke up this morning and found this card propped up on my keyboard. On the front it says: "I'm always telling other people how great I think you are." Open it up and it says: "Today I'm telling *you.*"

But listen to what he personally wrote: "Carrie, I'm so proud of your hard work. Thanks for giving our family an extraordinary life! Love, Eddie."

I will work way harder for an *extraordinary* life for my family than I will for money.

An extraordinary life means that last night at the dinner table our first-grader asked her dad if he would be her Room Dad. A lot of the other dads in town aren't involved in school at *all*, much less on a classroom level.

We live in a moderate- to low-income town with many of the dads working a lot of long hours and gone from home much of the time, as well as quite a few single-parent homes. She asked her dad if he would be the Room Dad and he had the luxury of saying yes. He was thrilled to be involved like that. He doesn't miss field trips, class parties, or school programs. Period.

We have the luxury of waking the kids up, snuggling, having breakfast, watching cartoons, packing lunches, dropping them off, and otherwise being involved in their lives. They aren't on a school bus in the dark or getting themselves ready while I commute to an office. Mr. Barefoot picks them up every day and they get out at different times, so he has date time, snack time, and catch-up time with them at the end of the day.

That's an extraordinary life because it's out of the ordinary, because it's not what other kids have. Another way we have an extraordinary life is that at Christmas we don't do piles and piles of presents; we travel. We have an experiential Christmas that's a priority to us.

Our children also have an extraordinary life because their grandparents live close by and on Fridays Baby Barefoot gets to hang out with the grandparents for a special date with them. I call that her "Fri-date." My parents are older and we waited so long to start our family and then spread them out so much that I really want her to have as much time with them as possible, because of the realities of their age and how time is so fleeting.

Those are some of the reasons that I do what I do, and you can tell I'm emotional about it. What I want you to know today is that you have to find out what you're so emotional about. My friend David Frey from Marketing Best Practices says, "Your *why* should make you cry."

You have to know why you're doing what you're doing. Working because you're out of a job, or working just to earn extra money, or working because you have this product in your head, that's not usually enough fuel to keep you going, to keep you motivated, to keep you persevering even when it's tough, even when you have obstacles.

When something seems optional, then we make it optional. But an extraordinary life for my family right now is not optional. It's what we've created for our four kids; it's what we've created for each other. We've surrounded ourselves with amazing people in this extraordinary life.

Take a minute right now and write down three ways you would like your life to be extraordinary.

- Would that mean a vacation every six months?
- Would that mean being able to drive your kids to and from school?
- Would that mean being debt free and being able to give to the charity of your choice without blinking, thinking, or budgeting?
- Would that mean being able to take care of your family or being able to help your brothers or sisters out in a time of financial crisis?

How would you like for your life to be extraordinary? Write it down.

_____

_____

_____

My great friend Frank McKinney, best-selling author of *The Tap, Make it Big*, and *Burst This!* said, "In order to have an extraordinary life, you must do things that are out of the ordinary. You must resist the ordinary path."

He speaks from experience. Frank builds $30 million homes on speculation on the coast of Florida, yes, even in this economy. Frank funds and builds entire villages in Haiti to house the poorest people on the globe. Frank has run the Badwater Ultramarathon in California's Death Valley—the world's toughest footrace—five times, and his last time was under forty hours for 135 miles. Few people can even complete this race. Frank has indeed resisted the ordinary.

Don't be ordinary today. Go a little above and beyond and be extraordinary. I believe you can. I believe you would love one of these notes propped up on your keyboard from somebody important to you.

BAREFOOT CASE STUDY

Steve Kloyda
Rosemount, Minnesota
TheProspectingExpertBlog.com
Sales and Prospecting Strategies

"Sales doesn't have to be hard or manipulative."

One of the first memories I have as a child, I was in third grade and I saw an ad in a magazine for a training course in art. The ad said, "Draw this lumberjack and send it to us." Well, I did. It was perfect. It looked exactly like the picture. My desire became to be an artist.

I graduated from the Minneapolis College of Art and Design but realized I had become an addict. So, I checked myself into rehab. After I left treatment, it was obvious to me that I wouldn't be creating art since the thought of painting terrified me. I just couldn't do it. It was time for a new life.

I was at the unemployment office looking for a new job when I saw this little tiny ad that read, "Stockbroker. Will Train. Call Tom, 338-1300." I thought, *Stockbroker. Wow! That could be me*. I applied for the job and begged to be hired. Little did I know how much Tom would change my life.

Everyone thought I was crazy. You—a stockbroker? What does that have to do with art? Absolutely nothing. Except that I could paint pictures over the telephone in the mind of the prospect about all the possibilities of the market. In my first eight months I opened up 180 new accounts. I remember opening up nine in one day. I broke every record month after month. I was on fire.

Funny thing, I switched my addiction to money. I couldn't make enough or spend it fast enough. I went for broke and that is where I ended up. I filed bankruptcy and lost everything of material value—house, cars, everything. What was I going to do? The most sensible thing I could think of was to start a business. Why not? What did I have to lose?

I started Telemasters, Inc., in 1990 and have since sold that name and brand and opened the Prospecting Expert, Inc., which clearly reflects my vision for prospecting strategies for the twenty-first century. I enjoy working with salespeople because so many of them were taught the wrong way to sell. It's a special gift to watch them grow and change when they learn that sales doesn't have to be hard or manipulative.

PART TWO RECAP

Mistake Number One: Pursuing something in which you have no experience and that is totally unrelated to your primary stream of income.

Mistake Number Two: Being distracted and developing too many ideas and income streams at one time. Focus on one priority until "positive cash" before you stray to another idea.

Mistake Number Three: Chasing hot trends, bright shiny objects, and functioning out of "opportunistic fear." *(What if I miss my chance at profiting at this? What if there is a limited window?)*

Those are the three that I see over and over again. If you have worked or studied with me at any point, you will see that pursuing any one of these three will not get you the results that you are seeking, whether that is consistent part-time income or radical full-time income.

The key to remember is that this is work and will take consistent quality effort on your part. I remember very clearly hearing Gillian Ortega say about her move from Ireland twenty years ago, "America is the richest, freest country in the world and you are blessed to be able to work, to build. Quit resenting that and embrace the gift that it is."

If you are still seeking the Easy button or the path to brainless riches, being self-employed is probably not the right road for you.

"That's not the path to freedom, that's just free dumb. You keep looking. You keep spending your money and keep trying to find the Easy button. If you find it, you let me know—meanwhile, I'll be over here working," said Paul Evans, PaulBEvans.com.

Part Three

The Methods

Six

The Mind-set of Success

A man must be big enough to admit his mistakes,
smart enough to profit from them, and strong enough to
correct them.

—John C. Maxwell

I have been working at home since the adoption of my eldest children in 1998, but I just entered the online business space in late 2007, after the birth of my fourth child. I kicked it into gear quickly because when you already have a profitable business that you are managing hands-on and four busy, beautiful children, you really don't have time to fiddle around.

How did I lose weight, get out of debt, succeed in business, take care of my kids, overcome depression, and basically reinvent myself? I attribute my "overnight success" to a few factors.

Your Mind-set

I'm not talking about reciting positive affirmations every day—"what you think about you bring about"—and all those kinds of things. Those are powerful strategies, but until you change your mind about who you are and whom you choose to impact and what you want to be and what you want to do, until you change your mind about it, you cannot achieve it.

Until you believe it, you cannot achieve it. You will never be thin until you believe that is a possibility. You will never be out of debt until you believe that you can make that happen. You will never be your own boss until you make up your mind to do it.

Do. Or do not. There is no "try."

—Yoda, *Star Wars*

So how do you lose weight or get out of debt? How do you achieve great things in your business? You have to believe you have the power to do it. One thing that I've noticed in almost every scenario I've been in lately with a group—whether it was my personal mastermind group or at a conference with amazing speakers or in a group of peers talking—is that we all tend to undervalue our own experience, our own gifts and skill sets that we bring to the world. We all tend to compare ourselves to the person on our left and the person on our right and the people sitting in front of and behind us. I am here to tell you that comparison is suicide on the installment plan. That isn't perhaps a politically correct phrase, but it's visually powerful and will help you understand how devastating comparison can be.

Quit comparing yourself to others. You need to focus on being *the best you* that you can be. That is the only comparison you should make. I want you to think in terms of a competitive swimmer. Competitive swimmers train hard, but when they train, they are beating their own best time. Runners do the same thing. That's how they know how to measure their improvements, because if you're winning a race with a lot of other slow people, that doesn't really make you fast. That doesn't really make you effective. It just makes you faster than mediocre, maybe.

You need to be *the best you* that you can be and realize that you are an expert. You are gifted. You are qualified and uniquely talented and called to do what you are going to do. So get over yourself. Get over wondering what everyone else is thinking and realize that they are thinking about themselves. They're not thinking about you. That's mind-set.

I had to believe when I was losing weight that it was one small choice at a time, one small action at a time. There was no "get-out-of-fat" free card. There was no "get-out-of-debt" free card or a "make yourself successful overnight" card. A lot of you are looking for "the answer," "the miracle," "the pill," or whatever it is. It's not there. If it were, I would be marketing that instead of teaching you how to better yourself.

Yes, pills are popular. Yes, surgery is popular. And I'm not going to debate any of those solutions. What I will say is that even with supplements, medications, machines, and surgeries, you still have to be in control of how you move your body and what you put into it. There is no "fix."

You have to quit looking for the magic and realize that the magic is in you. Go stand in front of the mirror and look closely. There's the magic. It is in you. It is not in anybody's program, service, or offerings. I firmly believe that one program, one course, one CD, one teaching can change your life *if* it helps you change your mind-set. I had to start thinking of myself as a thinner person. I had to start thinking of myself as a money student when I was so in debt, and I had to start thinking of myself as a business owner—and then I had to begin believing that I was a business grower, a woman who was intuitive in business and with finances. Many times you have to believe it before it can ever come to pass. Seems to be backward, I know. But it's true on so many levels.

Now here's the question: Are you thinking of yourself as a business owner, or are you thinking of yourself as someone who is trying a new "this" or attempting to make money doing "that"? Whatever it is, you need to be a business owner. As long as you keep playing at it, as long as you keep dabbling in it, until you fully commit—you will be in a hobby.

We all know that hobbies are usually not profitable. (Think of golf, sailing, fishing.) They're enjoyable, yes, but typically they cost you money. If you want to get really clear on the difference between a hobby and a business, ask the Internal Revenue Service. They have some guidelines they'd be happy to share with you.

My bottom line is that hobbies *cost* you money and businesses *make* you money.

So until you get a business motivation mind-set, you will likely not be as profitable as you can be. You have to get serious about it and get motivated and change your mind-set.

I think many times we are not hungry enough. What do I mean by that? I mean, kind of harshly, that as a society we are happy being discontent. We complain about our jobs, our mates, our homes, our bills, and even our hair. We are happy complaining. "Carrie, no, I'm not happy or I wouldn't be complaining!" Well, let me ask you—who does have the power to change your situation, if you don't personally?

This is what changed for me all those years ago. I made a choice to take my weight into my hands, my bills into my hands, and even my lack of employment into my hands.

Was it easy? No! But it was a simple decision. Enough was enough was enough, and until I was desperate enough, I was comfortable being discontent. And I believe this goes back to our initial "why"—until you know passionately and at a gut level why you are building a business or additional stream of income, you will be comfortable in your discomfort and all set to complain for the rest of your life.

A year ago I made up my mind that I was a speaker. I have spoken lots and lots, but I made up my mind that I was a speaker, a teacher, and a consultant. I made up my mind that I was a rock star businesswoman with something to offer to a larger audience. You must decide that you are a rock star, ready to fill your stadium with folks who are eager and ready to listen.

I love this sentiment: "You are an expert. Every fourth grader is a god to a third grader. Every third grader says: 'Wow. Look what all they know and what they can do. Look how high they can jump and how fast they can run.' You are the fourth grader to another third grader no matter what your niche, your market, your field, your avenue of income. You are a fourth grader to someone" (Perry Lawrence from AskMrVideo.com).

While we're talking about mind-set, let's also address the people you surround yourself with. You have to deflect negativity and absorb positivity. I probably made that word up, but that's okay. You understand what I'm saying. You have to deflect the bad and absorb the good.

You can say, "Oh, I'm strong and I can be a pillar for them." But the truth is, you are not deflecting their garbage, you are collecting their garbage. It will affect you at some point, whether you believe it or not.

The easiest way not to absorb negative energy is to stay away from it or ask people to respect your space. Say: "You know, that's really great. I am excited about what I'm doing, and I'm excited about what I'm achieving, and really I need your encouragement not your discouragement. I really need positive feedback at this point. I really feel that I need to surround myself with can-do type of people."

You have to train the people around you or limit the amount of time you're listening to them. Whether that's your mom, your closest friends, or someone else who is in business, hang with the striving not with the struggling. I'm not advocating that you ditch your parents or divorce your spouse, but you do need to be careful with whom and how you share your dreams and hopes. You also need to respect the "shareholders" (your immediate family) in your business. You need to be accountable to them on some level, but we'll address that in another chapter.

It is so important that you keep your mind clean. I don't watch or listen to the news, and I don't listen to negative people. I even will tell people: "That is really negative. I'm sorry, but I'm going to have to walk away because I really can't take that in because it affects me a lot. Let's talk about something different or something more positive." My assistant says it affects my mojo. She doesn't let me see a lot of negative e-mails because it affects my magic, my mojo.

My dad worries about the fact that I don't watch the news. He is concerned that a major disaster or crime wave will hit my area and I won't know. He calls me every once in a while and says, "I know you don't watch the news, so I just wanted to make sure you knew about the tornado that is three blocks away from you right now."

See? I'm covered. I'm not missing anything and I can stay positive.

You may think that it isn't realistic to avoid the negative or toxic people. But I intentionally purge people from my calendar and my headspace about quarterly. Sometimes it is difficult, but if we are really attempting something outside of the status quo, it is absolutely necessary.

You need to focus on what you're great at and what is positive because the negative can peck away at you. If you think about a vulture pecking away at the flesh on a dead animal—that is what negativity does to your spirit. It tempers how you look at yourself and how you function in your business. I want you to guard your mind and feed it with positive materials and even positive music rather than bad news and other negative

53

things. Maybe you won't choose to take as radical a stand as I do against negativity, but even if you make two or three intentional moves in that direction it will make a drastic positive change.

BAREFOOT ACTION STEP 1

Never, Never, Never Give Up!

The most essential factor is persistence—the determination never to allow your energy or enthusiasm to be dampened by the discouragement that must inevitably come.

—**James Whitcomb Riley**

Watch the "Never, Never, Never Give Up!" video at http://www.barefootexecutivevideos.com/persistence

Let's talk about perseverance.

Sometimes even the most positive of us, even the most profitable of us, gets a little discouraged. We come up to some roadblocks, some obstacles, some alligators, as I like to call them, and while we have really powerful whys, really powerful reasons why we want to achieve, sometimes it's easy to think about giving up on our dream.

This morning I read the story of Sylvester Stallone. I don't know if you know his story, but it really is amazing. He wanted to be an actor—he had a passion about being an actor. But a forceps injury at birth damaged part of his face.

We're all familiar now with the way his mouth curls and the way his speech is and the way his eye is, but he was told he couldn't act because people wouldn't want to look at him. He was literally broke, had sold his wife's jewelry, which officially ended their relationship, and had even sold his dog. He was at a really, really low point.

That dog was his best friend, but he sold his dog for twenty-five dollars outside of a liquor store. He was broke, he was down on his luck, and he went to the library and escaped for a little bit. He read a book that he credits with inspiring him to write—to express himself through the written word—and not give up.

A few days later, he watched a prize fight on television and within three days wrote the manuscript for *Rocky*. He felt so passionate about this story that he took it to several producers in and out of agencies. Finally he found someone who wanted to buy it for $125,000, but he wouldn't sell it unless the agreement included that he was to star in it.

They offered him $225,000 and he wouldn't sell it unless he starred in it. Even at $350,000 he wouldn't sell it because he passionately believed that he needed to play the lead character, Rocky Balboa. Finally the agency agreed to buy the script and let him star in it, but they lowered the amount to $35,000. He took it. The rest, as they say, is history.

I think the most incredible part of this story is that he went back to that same liquor store and waited for several days to meet the man who had bought his dog. He wanted his dog back. The man wouldn't sell him for twenty-five dollars or one hundred dollars. He sold him for fifteen thousand dollars, which was nearly half of what Stallone earned for the script. That dog stars in *Rocky*, right along with Sylvester Stallone.

But Sly believed in his dream; he would not give up. He would not give up on his dream; he kept at it. He kept writing, he kept pitching, he kept going in and out of those agencies and telling people about his dream and what he believed in. Are you willing to do that with your dream? Are you willing to do that with your business, with your product, with your service?

We all know the Sylvester Stallone who has starred in dozens of films, made millions and millions of dollars, and we're even familiar with his dog. When will we know about you? When will we hear about your dream and your successes?

I encourage you to keep at it today. Keep plugging even if today is a down day; even if today was a sell-your-dog day, keep at it. I believe in your dreams. You need to believe in your dreams as fiercely as Sylvester Stallone believed in his.

BAREFOOT ACTION STEP 2

Done Trumps Perfection, Every Time

So what do we do? Anything—something. So long as we don't just sit there. If we screw it up, start over. Try something else. If we wait until we've satisfied all the uncertainties, it may be too late.

—Lee Iacocca, former chairman of Chrysler

Watch the "Done Trumps Perfection, Every Time" video at http://www.barefootexecutivevideos.com/done

I actually gave this advice just a few minutes ago to one of my highest-level inner circle members.

He does really well, he has a really nice income, and he's growing in his business, but I've noticed during the last year that a couple of projects we've been working on together are always in progress or waiting on a programmer or waiting on something else. Some of those are very viable things.

But I said to him with a tiny bit of reproving, "You have a gift. You have a gift for overcomplicating some of these things. When I give you a simple idea or you have a simple idea, then you tend to overcomplicate it, add too many bells and whistles, too many features and benefits, too many things that then give you permission to delay the launch of that product or that service or that information."

His perfectionism is delaying his profit, and I'm wondering if you are having those same struggles. Don't overcomplicate what you are going to offer, don't overcomplicate what you're giving to customers, don't keep perfecting or adding to it. Sometimes enough is enough and we need to get it out there and see if there's an interest.

For instance, I have a course coming up and I really just want to get it out there. I don't have everything worked out to the nth degree, I don't have the multiple-pricing layers worked out yet, I don't have what I could add and develop worked out yet, but I'm going to go ahead and put the squeeze page or name capture form out there with a deadline, with an announcement to hold me accountable, to test the interest and see what's going on. This way I can build a list of interested parties or see if I should even waste my time on this project or interest.

This service that my client and I were talking about was going to be a really specific service, a narrow service that he was going to offer, and by the time he got the squeeze page up there were eight different options, four different pricing structures, and quite honestly I couldn't even look at the sales page without my eyes glazing over. It was too much and it took away from the niche—it took away from what he was specializing in.

Well, nobody wants to go to the dentist to deliver her baby; nobody wants the general practitioner to treat his cancer. We want a specialist. So don't be afraid to niche down; don't be afraid to keep things simple.

The last couple of weeks I've been testing this in a few different areas. I offered a simple product to my audience last week for $7—really simple information, but we made $2,500.

This week I tested the waters again with a different idea—somebody else's product for $15. Again, we did about $2,500 with that. If they had waited until they had multiple up-sells and backend and cross marketing and tweaks and bells and whistles, we'd still be waiting. But as a result they have $2,500 more in their pocket and so do I. So, quit delaying, quit giving yourself excuses to stop and to put it in somebody else's court. Set a firm deadline and keep it simple.

Here's my big strategy success secret. When you're working on many little projects, set a deadline on one. Pin yourself to the chair, don't open your e-mails, don't make any phone calls, don't schedule any appointments, don't go to the movies, don't take any time off, but focus for one full business day. Focus and say, "I'm not getting up out of this chair until this is done."

You will be surprised and shocked at how productive you can be when you do that.

A very common question is, "Carrie, what's your secret to implementing so many things at one time?" The fact of the matter is, I implement them one thing at a time in blocks and chunks of time. That's my secret, that's my strategy, and that's my challenge for you today.

BAREFOOT CASE STUDY

Jason O'Neil
Temecula, California
PencilBugs.com
15-year-old Author and Merchandiser

"It's never good to get too stuck on one goal because you might miss something else along the way."

I am only fifteen years old, but I've been in business since I was nine. Otherwise the life I have had has been very normal. I have attended regular schools, tried several team sports, performed in plays and talent shows, and have been entrepreneurial, which is what always set me apart from most other kids.

I started out with my Pencil Bugs products for kids, but my business has moved away from the product portion and moved into helping other people with their business ideas.

My mom encouraged me to come up with an entrepreneurial idea, which is what actually prompted me to make my bug-like pencil topper, which eventually turned into my business called Pencil Bugs. The reason I decided on a pencil topper was because I wanted to create a product that would make school and homework more fun for kids.

Because of manufacturing issues, there is a limited quantity of Pencil Bugs left, so those are staying in protective captivity. They may come back someday, but until then I hope to continue to inspire people through my book, *Bitten by the Business Bug: Common Sense Tips for Business and Life from a Teen Entrepreneur*, and also through speaking engagements. I promised the Pencil Bugs I would carry out their legacy in some way. I have other books in the works and am always open to opportunities that may pop up. I believe it's never good to get too stuck on one goal because you might miss something else along the way.

I live the life of a typical teenager. I go to school, do homework, play with friends, and soon I'll be playing tennis and in school musicals. I have daily chores that I need to do, like feeding the dog and helping around the house. I check my social networking sites and e-mails and often find people asking my advice on various things. In everything I do, I remember what my grandpa says, "Too much of a good thing can turn into a bad thing."

Seven

Take Massive Action

Make the decision. Without the decision, there is no action. Without action, there are no results. Without results, there is no success.

—Frederique Murphy, Mind-set Coach

I cannot think my way to the top of the stairs. I cannot think a hamburger into my hand. I have to take action to make those things happen. I have to believe it can happen in order to take the appropriate actions to get there. I hope that makes sense. I'm not dismissing the law of attraction, but, I'm saying back it up with action and it's a lot more powerful.

Now let's talk about massive action. I'm really fired up about this: Massive Action to Completion. So many of you have been studying for a really long time or thinking for a really long time. You are fixin' to get ready to get started to get goin'. You've been revving your engines. I'm here to tell you that you've got to put it in gear and get started. You've got to put it in gear and get out of the driveway. If you mess up or hit a bump and veer off path, it's okay. You're at least moving. When you're revving your engine, you're not getting anywhere. You're just making a lot of noise. I want you to quit making noise and start making tracks.

Even if you're messing up or you think that you're failing, a lot of you know that my favorite phrase is "Fail fast. Fail often. Success cannot elude you." You have to put your failures closer together. A lot of people get paranoid about the word *failure*. They say, "There's no such thing as a failure." Lighten up a little bit. I mean mistakes, missteps, and messes.

One of my vows is to turn every mess into a message and every test into a testimony so that you can learn as much from what I've messed up as you can from what I'm doing right. So get out there and don't be afraid to fall on your face.

Look at champion figure skaters. Look at champion hockey players or gymnasts or swimmers or football players. How many times have they missed? How many times have they fallen? How many bumps, bruises, and bloody knees have they had? A lot.

If you're afraid to make a mistake, you're afraid to live. If you're afraid to make a mistake, you're afraid to be great. You've got to get out there and get cut up a little. You've got to get out there and get wounded and sore. Bodybuilders don't get to where they are without tearing a few muscles or being sore—without having that workout hurt a little. But your muscles feel stronger and your form is better and you start being a little more competitive with every effort. If you only lift weights once every six weeks, you're not going to be a very competitive bodybuilder.

You've got to take massive action to completion. Don't start so many things at one time that you can't complete them—so many things at one time that it distracts you. You need to be focused and excited and directional. A broad beam does not cast as effective a light or stream as when it's more honed in and more narrowly focused—a laser beam.

Get focused on one thing, get it profitable and effective, get it to cash, and then you can focus on some of the other projects. Too many times we get so distracted by new offers and new strategies and new tricks that we say: *Oh, I want to do this and a little bit of this and a little of that. Wow. I have so many projects to do that I just can't focus right now.* Well, then how effective are any of them going to be? They're not.

My point is you have to focus. Get something you're doing and something you're excited about to cash—to profit—and success takes the stress off. Then you can pursue something that you're passionate about or that catches your attention while the other is still bringing in cash. Quit being so frazzled and get to the focus. A lot of times we're guilty of this because we are so great at multitasking. We are, and that's wonderful.

But sometimes multitasking affects the bottom line. The bottom line is going to be a little scattered if you're not focused, so my encouragement to you is to focus on the first project to cash.

Finding Your First Priority

The number one question I get is: "Carrie, I have so many ideas and so many that I know are going to be great. How do I know what to work on first?"

Okay, this is earth-shattering advice, so highlight it. Make a list of all your projects and products and things you want to develop. List them all, but not in any particular order. Just "brain dump." (That's a technical term.) You brain dump and write them all down.

Coaching Ideas

Finish e-book for low-price point offer	$1575
New group coaching program	$14,350
Live local workshop	$2000
Collaboration with Sharon	$7500

Then write how much money they can mean to you in the next thirty days. What kind of profit can you realistically expect in the next thirty days from each project? Write down the number.

Next—this is the important part—you reorder them in descending order so the one that will net you the most cash in the next thirty days is what you work on first.

Priority List

New group coaching program	$14,350
Collaboration with Sharon	$7500
Live local workshop	$2000
Finish e-book for low-price point offer	$1575

Then put your blinders on. Unless you already have a great team in place, put your blinders on and focus on the most profitable one.

Once you get that project to cash, you will have a little extra cushion, and you can perhaps delegate the one at the bottom of the list to somebody else. Pay somebody else to get your next project to cash while you're working on the second most profitable. Then you can meet in the middle maybe. Until you get the first one to cash, focus on it; then you can start working your way down the list.

That is my number one strategy for deciding what to focus on. What can you realize in thirty days from this project? Please, make the list. I promise you, it makes a difference. Working on what you are excited about or what is the "next big thing" is not going to improve your overall growth. You must focus on the list in priority order.

Now let's talk about motives.

I know we have lots of successful businesspeople reading this book. Lots of people already making money, and you have a lot of projects in the works too. That's great—then you decide what your motive is.

- Is your motive *immediate cash* in the next thirty days?
- Is your motive to generate as many *leads* as possible in the next thirty days?
- Is your motive *new appointments*?
- Is your motive *product creation*? *Systemization*?

Whatever your motive is, that's how you rank your priority list.

How many members will this project add to my membership program in the next thirty days? If that's your motive, then it isn't a dollar amount; it's a people amount. It's the same with lead generation. Then you rank them in descending order and do the same thing.

Whether cash is your focus or leads are your focus or it's speaking engagements—whatever your focus is in the next thirty days—you rank your projects in descending order on that list according to your motive. Too many times we think money is our motive and sometimes it's not. Sometimes it's leads or pages of a book you're writing or deadlines—you have to decide what your motive is and rank your priorities in that order. Massive action to completion.

Let me qualify a little bit. That is massive *appropriate* action. A lot of you are too busy being busy. The difference between business and busyness is the *i* and the *why*—what purpose are you working for? As long as you have your *why* in your business (not just the *y*), then you need to delegate out the busyness. You need to quit doing those avoidance behaviors. You need to quit doing the things that are not profitable and assemble some kind of virtual team or some kind of help with leveraging the people on your list or the people in your circle and focus on the things that are profitable and getting you closer to your "why."

You have to find out why you're taking massive action or your massive action just becomes busywork. I want you to keep that in the back of your head: Massive Action.

BAREFOOT ACTION STEP

Eliminate the Chaos!

Never again clutter your days or nights with so many menial and unimportant things that you have no time to accept a real challenge when it comes along. This applies to play as well as work.

A day merely survived is no cause for celebration. You are not here to fritter away your precious hours when you have the ability to accomplish so much by making a slight change in your routine.

No more busy work. No more hiding from success. Leave time, leave space, to grow. Now. Now! Not tomorrow!

—Og Mandino

**Watch the "Eliminate the Chaos!" video
at http://www.barefootexecutivevideos.com/clutter**

I'm a little casual today—jeans, T-shirt, ponytail, and kind of grubby. I've been cleaning out.

There's been some clutter in the house, some clutter in the office, on the shelves, and it just really was stifling me. At the same time I'm clearing out clutter on my calendar and clutter on my lists and it's restoring a state of calm and focus to what I'm doing.

Have you done that? Do you have clear goals written? Do you have clear tasks for every day written out? Do you have space that you can be calm in without looking around and thinking, *I have to do this. I have to do this. I have to do this*?

Part of that is delegation—things we can hand off to other people—but sometimes I think it's really just a matter of putting on your tennis shoes, an old T-shirt, and a ball cap, rolling up your sleeves, and clearing the clutter.

Maybe it's pinning yourself to the chair and cleaning some things off your to-do list that you've been putting off for long enough. Maybe it's a matter of making a list and sending it to your virtual assistant. Maybe it's sending it to someone on your team and letting that person handle it so you can clear it off. Sometimes it's a matter of getting the kids to help you clean out some things, take books to the library, take clothes out of the closet, take them to the clothing shelter.

How do you need to clean the clutter out of your life? Is it physical clutter? Are they courses you bought that you need to give yourself permission to either give away, sell on eBay, or take to the library?

Is it mental clutter? Things that you just won't release, maybe some good ideas that aren't quite profitable for you right now? Put them in an idea book and save them for later. Let go of them for now and focus on cash with your core business. How do you need to clean out the clutter?

I encourage you to take two hours and clean out your office, your desk, your drawers, your closet, your car. What do you need to clean out physically? Then I'm going to encourage you to take two hours and clean out the mental clutter, the emotional clutter, the to-do list clutter, and see if you can then take a deep breath, relax, and focus on what's important, focus on what's profitable, and focus on what's productive.

BAREFOOT CASE STUDY

Lain Ehman
Massachusetts
http://www.layoutaday.com
Scrapbooking

"No one thing is going to make or break you as a businessperson."

I have an undergrad degree in public policy from Stanford and a master's in public administration from Syracuse. I worked in government for several years and then in PR before becoming a freelance journalist in 1997 when my son was born. I became involved in scrapbooking around that time, and after the birth of my two other children, I thought I should try to meld my love of scrapbooking with my journalism career. I eventually became an editor and instructor for one of the major scrapbooking magazines, and even wrote a book and contributed to several more. Then the economy crashed, the magazine folded, and I looked around and thought, *I'm on my own, baby!*

I never really enjoyed working for someone else—too much focus on how many hours you put in rather than how much you produced—so I thought I'd see what I could do online. I had a pretty good following in scrapbooking because of the books, the magazine, and teaching—so I wanted to find a way to monetize that so I would never *(never!)* have to go back to an office again.

My husband has a great job that takes care of all our basics, but we wanted more—private school, vacations, fun stuff—and that all comes from my business and me.

I started my own business in 2010.

Scrapbookers spend their time creating physical representations of the people and things they love. They're creative, supportive, and—at least in my community—funny and fun to be around. They notice the little things about life and want to make their world a better place.

Things change too much to predict what will happen next month, let alone next year. I do know that I love the freedom, flexibility, and fun that an online business offers me. I truly am my own boss. As I move more into creating passive income, my days will change even more.

Typical doesn't exist for me. I work six to eight hours a day, but not all at once. I break it up, do some in the evening, read while the family is watching a movie or working on homework, etc.

I enjoy the challenge of building something useful and valuable from nothing. Everything my company is came directly from my hard work— that's simply amazing to me. I am very results driven, so looking at my community and being able to say, "I created this!" is a huge rush for me. I would say I'm equally driven by the money and the recognition.

My focus is on *fun*. Some people take scrapbooking way too seriously. I figure, if it isn't fun, why do it? I put a lot of personality in everything I do, whether it's a video series or a short tweet. I try to add life and energy and humor to people's lives.

But I want to quit every time I hit a technology demon. I try to "talk myself off the ledge" by convincing myself there has to be a way to do it and I just can't see it. This is when I turn to a business coach, community, or other adviser. Often I'll willingly pay someone to do what I want to get done.

I wish someone had told me a year ago that no one thing is going to make or break you as an online businessperson. If one thing doesn't work, there are other ways to make money. If one plug-in doesn't do it, there's another. Just keep picking at the knot until one little part gets unraveled.

Eight
Masterminding

The third key has been huge for me. It is masterminding. I joined my first mastermind group in 2008, and it has tripled my income. It has more than quintupled my contacts and the people I know and my speaking engagements, as well as how big I think. It's also where I met Paul Evans, the cofounder of 100xMissions (www.100xMissions.org), that I'm such a passionate supporter of now. It's where I met some of my very best friends and powerful allies in business.

As a disclaimer, I will tell you I have two such mastermind groups that I facilitate. I also have made it a permanent part of my business plan to be a part of a group that I don't personally lead. Yes, I pay to be in a group even though, by all counts, my business is doing really well.

The power of a mastermind is huge. A mastermind is a group of like-minded people who are possibly all in different niches or different business models, but you bond or bind together to brainstorm each other's businesses to say: "Here's what's working in my business. Here's what I need help on. Here's who I know that you should know. Here's who I'm connected to that you should know. Here are some things you should implement that I think would be amazing for you. Here's an idea. I got it at another conference. It doesn't fit me, but it might be great for you."

This is the synergy of an amazing group. Why is a mastermind necessary? The truth is, you're intelligent and driven. You are savvy and can figure this out on your own and be in business by yourself if you want to. That's fine. That's a model a lot of people use. But I prefer to be in business for myself but not *by* myself. I prefer to have a brain trust, if you will—a group of people who have me on their radar all the time thinking of how we can impact and benefit each other—and brainstorm.

A mastermind is huge. We will be sitting there brainstorming and come up with ideas for creating software, phone apps, generators—things that none of us necessarily would've thought of before. Napoleon Hill in his classic, *Think and Grow Rich*, calls it "the power of the third mind."

When you form a mastermind of powerful people who have a vested interest financially and time-wise in the group, then there's a third mind that mysteriously appears of joint ideas you wouldn't have had on your own. It's hard to explain until you experience it, but it's a powerful thing. You need to surround yourself with like-minded people for exponential growth.

The late business and personal-growth expert Jim Rohn emphatically believed that "your income will be like the five people you spend the most time with." So if you aren't happy with your income, look at where you're hanging out. Look at whom you see and whom you're noticing. Look at whom you're talking to on the phone and whom you're e-mailing the most. Who is taking your energy and who is giving you *theirs*?

The people around you should evolve if you're growing. If your group doesn't evolve and grow with you, then you need to get a different group. Then you need to choose some more friends—not saying you have to leave your old friends behind, but you have to be careful about where you're investing your time and your energy. I'm serious. It makes a huge difference.

I can look back over the last ten years of my life and with every big growth or change, every big leap in my life, every mind-set change, every income spurt, every period of growing and stretching, my peer group has changed. My closest friends have changed. The people around me can either grow with me or get left behind because I'm not willing to be one of those people who complains ten years from now about the same things or deals with the same obstacles and issues that they're dealing with now. I don't even want people to be able to say that I'm complaining about the same obstacles or issues of a year ago or even six months ago.

I want people to say: "Wow. I can hardly keep up with her—with her ideas and business growth, with her attitude, or mind-set." I want people to know that I'm in a constant state of growth and change and excitement and adventure in life, business, and family.

You need to surround yourself with those kinds of people. One of the most exciting things about live events and online masterminds and even social networking is that you can find a group of like-minded people, a group of your "peeps" (that's what I call people who know what you're talking about—people who are challenged with what you're challenged with and deal with the same things). It's so nice; it's a safe place to grow.

You need to make sure that you are consciously putting yourself in the right atmosphere and habitat for you to grow professionally, physically, and emotionally. It's a biblical life concept. You have to plant yourself in the right soil or your talents will return void. It's been proven that it's just the truth of the matter. You need to choose a wise mastermind or accountability group.

Let me tell you a little bit about the benefit of a paid mastermind versus an unpaid mastermind. When we throw our money over the bar, our hearts tend to follow. When we commit with our paycheck, our pocketbooks, our credit cards, an investment—when we invest in a group like that, we tend to be more committed. That's the bottom line.

I committed to my first mastermind group to the tune of $15,000 that I did not have—luckily, there was a payment plan. My husband (typically the more financially conservative of the two of us) convinced me by saying: "Carrie, if you get one idea from this mentor, this coach, from someone in this group, can you make back that $15,000 this year?"

Well, that was like a challenge to me. Like saying "sic 'em" to a bulldog, as we'd say here in the South.

I said, "Absolutely I can."

He said, "Then is it worth your time for one idea?"

effort into your life and into your business and your results are directly correlated to those efforts.

If you're putting peanut butter and jelly in your lunch box, that's what you're going to get. If you're putting inconsistent, spotty, halfhearted, maybe-this-might-work effort into your business, those are the kind of results you're going to get.

If you're a "zoom-eeker," meaning you go whole hog for your business *zoooom* and then you slam the brakes on—*eeeeek*—and you question and you self-doubt and then you zoom again, you're never going to have the results that you want.

I challenge you to make a different lunch and to be consistent with quality effort. Know that just as our moms always said, "Garbage in, garbage out"—quality in, quality out; consistency in, consistency out.

You are the one who's packing your lunch for your business. What will you find when you open your lunch box?

BAREFOOT CASE STUDY

Nicola Bird
London
www.JigsawBox.com
Life Coach

"It was only when I started working with a coach myself that my business really took off."

When I decided that I wanted to dictate my own working hours and set out to find a business I could run by myself, I sat down with a friend, and we came up with a list of my primary skills. There was only one. Being bossy. We decided that there must a career path where that would be considered an attribute, and came up with teaching or coaching. I read a book on coaching, and although it was the complete antithesis of being bossy, I fell in love with the practical, pragmatic nature of coaching and I trained as a life coach.

I started out coaching women who'd recently had small children, but because I was in the same situation, I found my clients often had children who were asleep when mine were awake, or they would have to cancel appointments because their kids were sick (or mine were). When I came across the idea of coaching my clients online, I could immediately see the benefits to me and my clients.

I started to coach my clients in writing, online; however, I soon realized that the system I was using didn't do what I wanted to do. I thought, *I can do this better myself* and hired two freelancers to build me the prototype of what eventually became JigsawBox, my own online coaching tool.

I launched it, and thirty coaches signed up right away. I took it down again and brought in some new developers in New Zealand, who then built me a more advanced version of my original idea. More and more coaches were attracted to the tool as a way of teaching their clients and then coaching them to apply what they'd learned to their own circumstances, so again, we invested a whole heap of money into the business and completely built the application from scratch to give us the tool we have today. We currently have around five hundred coaches using JigsawBox to package their expertise and sell it online.

So I run JigsawBox with my team, but I also spend a large chunk of my time coaching others to use JigsawBox to grow their own coaching businesses and to create and market ways to sell more than their one-on-one time. That's because I'm a mother of three young children, and I want to spend time with *them* and still get paid, not fill my diary with one-on-one clients.

I love providing JigsawBox because the coaches who come across it have never seen anything like it before and they get *really* excited about the concept of selling more than their time and achieving the results and lifestyle I have by using the tool.

I also have a passion and have set a goal for helping one thousand coaches help one thousand people each. The majority of the work I do is with coaches who want to create their first $50K—to get over that first tough bit of building their businesses successfully. I love working with these people because they each have a unique gift to bring, and it frustrates me when they just don't know how to get it out there.

I'm more of an entrepreneur than a coach, and I have a business, not a job. So I don't see my business running the way it does now forever; however, I do always see myself being a business owner. I *love* the fact that you get to decide how much you want to earn and then go do it! I love it when a new sale comes into the business. I love the fact that a by-product of what I do is that more coaches help more clients.

There are many "whens" with running your own business: When we get hundreds of questions on the support desk for JigsawBox I think, *There has to be an easier way!* When I launch a product and no one buys it, I want to quit. When I launch a teleseminar and the technology lets me down, I'm frustrated. When I do a promotion and people send me nasty e-mails telling me to stop sending them more, it's disappointing. When everyone around me was asking when the money was going to start coming in, I faced a little fear. When the only way to grow is to do something totally scary and I don't want to, I have to dig for courage.

I spent the first two years of my business life as a coach without a coach of my own. Looking back, I thought, *I can't afford it,* but I now know that's just daft. That was one of the costliest decisions I ever made, as it was only when I started working with a coach myself that my business really took off. That was two whole years of not earning *any* money when I could have been—what a waste! But really I have no regrets because if I'd done anything differently, I wouldn't be where I am right now, and I couldn't really ask for more.

Nine

Finding a Mentor

A s I talk to you about the power of mentors, I'll use a story about my dad to tie the points together.

My dad, Robert Owensby, modeled this concept for me very powerfully over and over in my life. He was in the Coast Guard for twenty-seven years. I'm very proud of him. Now he's been in the ministry for just as long. He is more than seventy years old and can do anything, but he wasn't born that way.

He was actually raised in an uneducated family. My grandfather was verbally abusive and an alcoholic for many years. College was not discussed, and as a matter of fact, my dad was the first high school graduate on either side of the family.

My dad demonstrated an indomitable spirit and a "can-do" attitude. He decided early on in his life that there was nothing he could not figure out. He decided that other folks might have more money but no one had more will than he did.

I could list dozens of examples, but one in particular is my favorite. When I was about seven years old, we moved into a home in Elizabeth City, North Carolina, that was very small. This was a military transfer and my dad preferred to live off base and have our own home.

But this house was very much in line with his salary—not his family size. There were three kids, around eleven years old and under, and my mom and dad. Quite frankly, the house was too small. My dad told my mom that we were going to put on a second story. She said, "We don't have the money for that." He told her it was okay, that he was going to build it. She said, "You're a flight engineer. What do you know about contracting?" He told her he had just ordered a series of books.

He ordered the Time-Life Home Improvement series. They were hardback books. They're what I call the original continuity membership program. You received one book every three weeks or so. One was on roofing. One was bricklaying. One was on plumbing, one on electricity—you get the idea. My dad had the attitude that if it was in a book, he could do it.

Let me tell you, my dad put a second story on that house—he added two bedrooms and a bathroom. He also added a second living area with a beautiful fireplace, a party patio with a sunken fire pit, and a flight of stairs. I thought he was magical. He even built a room under the staircase so my mom could have a sewing room. He transformed that house with his hands.

Was it perfect? No. I remember that the boys were delayed in getting to move upstairs because the book on plumbing or electricity (I don't remember which one) hadn't come yet, so he couldn't finish. I remember that he took the roof off the house and it rained. We were a little wet, but he was determined that he was going to build the house with what was in those books. He took action.

Were those books magical? Did Time-Life have a magic secret? No, the magic was in my dad and his ability and willingness to take action. He learned from other contractors—other people. He would say: "I'm doing this and this. What am I doing wrong? What has been your experience?" He learned from mentors—a group. He learned from that product he purchased. He was instilling in me that you don't have to have it all figured out. He didn't wait until he had the whole series of books. He didn't wait until he had read everything and practiced on everything. He took massive action right then to completion using the information he had and drawing upon the resources of those around him.

I couldn't be more proud of him. Now, thirty years later, he leads teams into disaster-ravaged areas to rebuild after hurricanes, tornadoes, and flooding—with those skills he learned.

Do you think he knew that new homes in New Orleans, new churches in Galveston, or new orphanages in Africa and Russia were in that box of books when he ordered them off the TV advertisement? Do you think the developers of the Time-Life Home Improvement series ever had any intention of affecting orphans worldwide or hurricane victims? Probably not—but the magic was in my dad and in what he chose to do with that investment.

You have magic in you. But no one can unearth it except you.

Honestly, my family probably didn't have the money for that book subscription. We were living very much paycheck to paycheck. My mom was a stay-at-home mom. She was committed to being with us every moment. While she always leveraged her skills for extra money from piano lessons, sewing, or crafting, Dad was the primary provider for our needs. And being an enlisted officer with three young children, that was a stretch. In order to be a wise steward of that investment, he had to take massive action—immediate action—and action to completion. He taught me that by modeling it. I have no excuses. He had a full-time job and built a home on the side—how crazy is that?

I feel the same about my business and what I invest in and what I put into action. I challenge you to do the same thing. I love to work with people who have no excuses or "victim-itis"—no reasons why they can't succeed—only reasons why they must succeed.

We needed a bigger home. He wanted more space for his kids to grow. He wanted privacy for him and Mom. And so he made it happen. Period. Yes! It really *can* be that simple! My dad has never made very much money. From the military to the ministry, we've always been provided for, but never wealthy. But in my opinion, my dad is the most successful person I've ever met.

That being said, I think you determine what your measure of success is.

- You may be excited about $200 to $500 a month. That's amazing and that could change your financial picture, and I know that.

- You may be excited about $2,000 to $5,000 a month. That's amazing and I can encourage you to do that and show you how to do that.
- You may want to make $200,000 to $500,000 a year, and that is certainly possible and achievable. I can challenge, mentor, and coach you to those income levels.
- You may want to be a seven-figure earner. It's possible. Yes, you can do that from home. I mastermind and mentor with people who do that.
- You may be okay with your current income level except that you are in an excessive amount of debt. You may just want to wipe your debt clean and use your business for that only. I get that too!

I never intended to position myself as a mentor. I thought, *Who am I to position myself as someone to be looked up to?* You could learn so much from so many other people. But I've been put into this position because of experience, example, mind-set, and having been mentored myself. Here's what I will tell you. You need to find a mentor. You need to consciously choose a mentor. Whether you follow mentors virtually or are in their space physically, whether or not you pay to be part of their group, you need to consciously choose mentorship.

I've read books by people and modeled my behavior after them. I've followed some people online and modeled my business strategies after them, but what I try to do is choose one person at a time so that I'm not confused about all the conflicting messages that I hear.

I chose my first online business mentor very carefully. I worked with Yanik Silver and paid to be part of his group so that he would mentor me. He has small children like I do. He believes you need to still have fun in your business. He works from his home, and he has a virtual staff like I do. He is also very passionate about giving forward to causes he is excited about, and as you know, that really resonates with me.

So I thought there was a lot I could learn from him. He is one year younger than I am. He's had a phenomenal amount of success online. He also was in business offline with his dad for years, so I knew he would understand the model I was after. I knew he could teach me shortcuts and things he had experienced. It's just as important that somebody can teach you things not to do as that they can teach you what to do.

I invested heavily to be in Yanik's mastermind group and be mentored by him. Am I'm telling you to go spend $15,000? No. I'm telling you this because I'm telling you my story, and I consciously chose that particular mentor.

Working from home can be a challenge. Having dealt with both offline and online business can be interesting. Even though Yanik and I have many things that are different about us, we also have many things that are the same. I felt that I could learn a lot from him. We have continued our business relationship and friendship beyond the borders of that group and have even raised funds together for Frank McKinney's Caring House Foundation for a safer and healthier Haiti. There are so many benefits from being intentional and conscious about your mentor choice.

Now I'm coaching and mentoring with someone else. I choose very strategically, based on business model, family style, and position in the industry. Don't be mentored just because they're making good money, they're in your same industry, or they have the same type of family as you. Choose your mastermind group, your mentor consciously—purposefully, with great deliberation.

- Choose somebody who resonates with you.
- Choose somebody whom you can introduce to your mother and your children.
- Choose somebody you enjoy spending time with.
- Choose somebody who is like-minded with your core beliefs.

I have also coached and mentored with Dan Sullivan from Strategic Coach and with Zig Ziglar. They served very different purposes and roles in my business growth. But growth is key. This is a hard road to venture alone.

Then when you invest with a coach, consultant, or strategist, make sure you're bringing your part to the table. A coach cannot do batting practice with you if you aren't a willing participant. He can throw the ball at you. If you don't swing or have your glove on, you can't hit or you can't catch. You have to be willing to catch the ball, hit the ball, or toss it back before the coach can show you ways to be more effective in your game.

Why is a coach or a mentor a necessary part of your business? Ask Michael Jordan if he would be without his coach. Michael Jordan is arguably the best basketball player of all time, and he says that a coach is vital to him because a coach can see things in his game that he's blind to. A coach sees him play from a different view and can help him in ways that he's too passionate or too close to. A coach can help him see objectively.

Ask top dancers, vocalists, actors, or peak executives whom they coach with. I promise you, they are studying with someone and modeling after someone.

The most famous businesspeople in the world have business coaches and advisers. They have people who help keep them in check and are able to see things from a different viewpoint. That is why a coach, mentor, and mastermind are so valuable. You can see how these three things all work together.

A coach is not going to do you any good if you don't practice. A mentor won't do you any good unless you have the right mind-set and you're taking massive action to completion. And unless you're surrounded with a peer group that is supportive and working with you, you won't succeed.

This concept was driven home to me while I was watching *Cinderella Man* with my husband. Russell Crowe stars in this true story about a down-on-his-luck boxer. I've always thought that the "guy in the corner" was primarily for shooting water on the face and in the mouth of the fighter and for putting his silky robe on him. Not so.

What became apparent to me was that the "guy in the corner" could see the fight in a very different way than the boxer could. The boxer is too close to see where the punches are coming from or where they will land.

Having someone in your corner who has not only reviewed films of other fights but also can see from an objective perspective is *key*. I won't spoil the end of that film for you, but being able to "see" through that lens of "when you swing right, he always goes for the kidney" or "this is the series of punches he uses when he has you against the ropes" can give you an advantage you wouldn't have if you were just swinging reactively and hoping a punch will land somewhere, somehow.

BAREFOOT ACTION STEP

What Is Your Skunk?

Entrepreneurs are simply those who understand that there is little difference between obstacle and opportunity and are able to turn both to their advantage.

—Attributed to Niccolo Machiavelli

**Watch the "What Is Your Skunk?" video
at http://www.barefootexecutivevideos.com/skunk**

If you've watched my videos, you know I'm a country girl. You can probably tell by the accent and the fact that I'm barefoot most of the time. My office is on my property, but I have to go through a little walk-through to get there, out my back door and across a little path. Today, there was literally a skunk outside the back door.

I couldn't get outside of my house to get to my office. I had a very real obstacle between where I was and where I wanted to be and it was a really smelly, threatening kind of obstacle. Now, the fact of the matter is, I wasn't in danger, it wouldn't have hurt me probably, and it might have been just as scared as I was, but I didn't want to get all stinky and smelly and yucky in the process if I scared it.

So I let that come between what I needed to do and me. I waited some time; I went to the other end of the house and turned on some lights and made some noise out the side door, trying to distract the skunk so it would go away. The truth is we all have skunks—we have something between where we are and where we want to be, where we need to be.

We are allowing what my friend Zig Ziglar calls "stinking thinking." We are allowing either stinking thinking or something from our past or some fear of responsibility, fear of success, fear of failure, fear of I don't know what. I can't explain what your block is, what your skunk is, I only know what mine have been in the past. Let me give you some examples.

In dealing with weight loss, sometimes we sabotage success because we don't like attention. The first time somebody compliments us or gives us unwanted attention or we feel threatened in any way or maybe the first time our spouse gets jealous or somebody makes a snide remark, such as, "You just think you're cute" or "Don't get too skinny," the first time that happens, we start to sabotage our weight loss. We struggle with the fear of success.

Maybe our families have always been in a certain income zone, so we sabotage ourselves unconsciously before exceeding that income, or sometimes we exceed it and then we sabotage ourselves right back down because our family has always struggled or always just had enough, or we have some thoughts or feelings about wealth.

I don't know what's blocking you, I don't know what your skunk is, but I know that until you see it, until you recognize that it's there and until you think of a way to draw it out of your path, it's always going to block you from where you want to be.

I challenge you to take five minutes today to identify your skunk. I know this is revolutionary teaching, right? Identify your skunk and then think of how you can draw it out of your path so you can go around it or go over it or go another route to where you want to be.

BAREFOOT CASE STUDY

Jane Button
Washington
design2marketsuccess.com
Consultant and Coach for Creative Products

"It bothers me when people think they are stuck in a job. If they only knew the opportunities that await if they just started somewhere."

My grandfather was a huge inspiration to me. At the age of sixty-five, he retired as director of advertising for a major corporation and opened a small gourmet kitchen shop, one of the first of its kind before Williams Sonoma and the big celebrity chef craze. He took his advertising and used it to communicate with customers, and people in our community (Wilmington, Delaware) were avid consumers. I used to follow him around or drive him around when he designed products or bought them. My grandmother was also instrumental—she taught me to sew and knit. My sister and I had little "toy" Singer sewing machines, and we learned to make doll clothes at a very young age. I had no idea how these skills would put me into business years later.

At the time I started my business I was married with two young children. I had no background for business at all—I did not know or understand what "cash flow" meant. I just did it and learned how along the way.

I started my business because my husband and I disagreed on spending the money to send our two young children to private school. So I said I'd start a business and I'd pay for it! Little did I know at the time how it would change my life. I decided the traditional working for someone else would just not do for me—I wanted to be at home with our children and make money. I figured I could decide my income by creating a product. So—that's what I did.

After a series of misses and a few craft shows where I was selling one thing at a time, I decided to sell direct to stores. The first one I approached liked my knitted hat designs and I was in business. I then went on to other small boutiques and Nordstrom. They all bought. And the next year when I approached Nordstrom again, they wrote me an order for $40K—this put me over the top and it's when I really knew I had real business. I had to hire people to knit, and I had to find the money and put together a plan.

I did it—and that summer my husband was diagnosed with a brain tumor. Over the next three years we lived with our "feet planted firmly in midair." My husband and father of my children died at the age of forty. I was in my mid-thirties, a widow with two young children. I had a choice to make—I chose being an entrepreneur. Over the course of the next fifteen years I turned my little cottage industry into nearly a five-million-dollar company selling to all the major department stores and boutiques throughout the United States.

Starting your own business is life changing; it is a huge self-help and growth course. I love helping people make a living doing what they love. It bothers me when people think they are stuck in a job. If they only knew the opportunities that await if they just start somewhere.

I can't see myself not being an entrepreneur—ever! I sold my first business and went on to start another one in a completely different industry that became a seven-figure business. Now my primary business is helping other people do what they love with creative products—taking them to market and learning how to make money with their creativity.

In a way it was good that I did not know everything when I started because I might have been too scared—or I might have thought I didn't know enough. I really just did it and had no idea what I didn't know.

Ten

Do Your Research

Good fortune is what happens when opportunity meets with planning.

—Thomas Edison

I want you to type in a couple of your key words. For example, if you decide you want to focus on helping people lose more than one hundred pounds, type "lose more than one hundred pounds" into Google.com or your favorite search engine. (Type in whatever you think your audience might be looking for.) See what other Web sites come up.

Go into Amazon.com and do the same thing. See what books come up. Go to iTunes. See what podcasts come up. Go to blogtalkradio.com. See if any shows come up. Go to YouTube and see what videos come up.

If there are several entries, then you don't say, "Oh no! Somebody else is doing it." You say, "Wahoo! People want what I have—there is a market." We can get you into that market base too. Okay?

Don't get caught up in it or discouraged and don't buy anything. But ask, "How can I do that differently? How would I do that better? How would I have answered that question differently on my blog?"

Details

You need to consider, for example, how you will structure your business. Are you going to structure it as a sole proprietorship, a corporation, a limited liability corporation, or a partnership?

But the majority of us simply need to make the decision to be a business owner and decide what we're going to focus on. Then we focus on which model we're going to pursue first, how we're going to charge, as far as ongoing retainers, per transaction, or onetime. And then we'll talk about revenue streams: which revenue streams will we incorporate after we become profitable?

Rather than getting hung up on the proprietorship and the corporation and structural details—I suggest that you go to your county clerk's office and get a DBA, a "doing business as" certificate. A DBA certificate usually costs twelve to twenty-five dollars. It's pretty fast to get it, and it allows you to open a bank account in the name of your company, which allows you to have a checkbook, and that's a first step in getting your PayPal account or your merchant account set up so you can process credit cards.

These are some of the very basic steps, the first mapping you need to do before you can go any further. It's part of business. It's a very, very important foundation. Don't get hung up on your logo or on your business cards. The Barefoot Executive was three years in business before we had an official logo, and yet we still did loads of business.

Deadlines

Let me encourage you to set a deadline for implementing the things in this book. Quickly move through these exercises and these beginning steps for business building in four weeks (or if you already have a business, I suggest you focus on growth and implementation for four weeks). And I want to encourage you that for four weeks, you can do anything.

Yes, you can do anything for four weeks.

I remember that as a newlywed, one summer I worked eighty-five hours a week. I'm not exaggerating, I really did. It was brutal, but I kept saying, "I can do anything for these couple of months. This is going to help me pay off my student loans. I can do anything for these couple of months."

My last summer and the fall semester of college, I decided I was ready to be completely finished, so I took eighteen hours during the summer sessions and twenty-seven hours in the final fall semester so I could graduate at Christmas. (I don't recommend that, but I did it, graduated with honors, and my husband got chicken pox and missed my graduation. True story.)

Think of a new mom who typically goes without good sleep for at least six to eight weeks.

Think of a college student who is going through that last semester of lots of papers or exams, or even pledge week during fraternity/sorority season.

Think about other difficult seasons in your life. Maybe an illness or maybe a time on bed rest, or maybe just a really tough, busy time with your kids or with your spouse traveling. Think about military spouses whose husbands or wives are gone on a tour. Think about military boot camp.

You can do anything for four weeks. And I want you to pour your heart, your soul, your energy, your belief, your focus into this area of your business—and that is the area of growth.

Sometimes when we're stalling or we feel like we're blocked or we're not making the progress we want to, it is because we don't have a focus or a commitment. So I want you to focus. I want you to commit to four weeks of business building.

Building the Right One for You

Your Turn

Here are some idea exercises for you.

Where Are You Spending Money?

When you have discretionary money, what do you spend money on? Depending on the audience, it might be golf, it might be fishing, it might be a self-growth book, it might be jewelry making or bead stringing. It might be embroidery patterns or business books or software programs or business tools.

What do you spend money on when you have discretionary income? Write down three of those things right now.

_____

_____

_____

What Are Your Interests?

What do you read about? When you pick up a magazine or when you buy a book, what are you reading about?

What are some of your interests that you read about and spend your time immersed in? List those things here.

_____

_____

_____

What Did You Excel at in School?

Here's another fun question. When you were a kid, maybe in elementary school or junior high or maybe even high school or college, what did you excel at? What made you feel successful?

Maybe it was a certain subject area, maybe it was student government, maybe it was theater, or maybe you excelled at teaching other kids some of the basic principles. Maybe you excelled at writing.

What did you excel at when you were younger? Go ahead and list two or three of those things.

_____

_____

_____

What Do People Bug You About?

What do you get asked questions about? Maybe questions your neighbors or your friends or other people you work with ask. What are some of the most common questions you are asked?

For instance, when I had my publishing company and I was working at home, nobody else I knew was working at home unless they were in the direct sales industry. The questions I got all the time were:

- "How do you make money at home?"
- "How do you keep from feeling lonely?"
- "How do you handle your taxes?"
- "How do you connect with other people?"
- "How do you get new clients?"

Those questions were things I was asked all the time, so I answered them over and over and over again. Then I discovered that I was teaching.

What are you asked about all the time? Here's a little tip: Look in the sent file of your e-mail account. What kind of e-mails are you answering frequently? On your Facebook, what kind of questions are you answering? Think back to your phone conversations. What are people asking your advice about? Kittens? Weight loss? Organization? Healthy cooking? Living on a budget? Do your kids have great manners? Homeschooling? Having a full CPA practice? Being a profitable lawyer without being sleazy?

A friend and client of mine, Barry Chandler, teaches bar and restaurant owners to be more profitable at TheBarBlogger.com. And he is really great at telling other bar owners which drinks are most profitable, what are the most profitable times of day, what are the good lead-ins, how to make your establishment most profitable. So now he has a business doing that—globally.

What Questions Are You Asked?

What are you asked questions about the most? List them.

_____

_____

_____

What Interests You?

What are some things that have always intrigued or interested you? Write those down.

_____

_____

_____

What Entertains You?

What are some of your hobbies? Write them down.

_____

_____

_____

What Are You Chatting About?

What do you find yourself talking about when you're in groups or at parties or maybe at church or PTA meetings? What do you talk about that you get really fired up over? What do you and the guys or girls talk about at the gym? What do you and friends discuss over coffee? Pay attention. Maybe your energy changes, your voice raises pitch, the speed that you're talking gets a lot faster. What are you talking about a lot? Is it politics? Is it parenting? Is it shopping? Is it travel? What do you talk about a lot? Write it down.

_____

_____

_____

What Are You Trained For?

What have you had special training in? Have you had speed-reading? Speed-typing? Have you had foreign language training? Have you had training in language skills? Software training? Landscape artistry? Construction? Room design? Write five to seven things that you've been trained in. And I mean like a school course or maybe your degree or a continuing education course or something at college you studied or something your job required you to do. (Maybe you even learned from your mom or dad.)

_____

_____

_____

All right. Can you think of any more? Were you trained in any special process or any special coaching or counseling? Do you have any certification—even online certification? Any offline certification? Do you have any special licenses? Yes, CPR counts. Add them to your list above.

What Makes You Smile?

Write down some things that make you smile. Just asking you that question makes me smile.

_____

_____

_____

Review Your Lists

Look back over your lists. Those are skills, gifts, talents, things that set you apart. Guess what? You _rock_! (I can't even see your lists and I can tell you that!)

Now I'm going to add one more section. Let's depart from the external and go internal.

Have You Had Pain?

What extremely painful experience have you been through? Depression? Anorexia? Getting laid off? Divorce? Losing a parent? Losing a child? Being overweight? Illness? Maybe you've been abused as a child or as a young adult or as a spouse. Maybe you've been abandoned. Maybe you've been betrayed somehow. Maybe you've been passed over for a job. Maybe you didn't get a part you auditioned for that you had your heart set on. Maybe you've been in a tremendous amount of debt. Maybe you've been through infertility. You can write down several painful experiences. Nobody's going to see this but you, unless you choose to share, so write down several, right now.

_____

_____

_____

I know we tend to mask these things and think we don't want to incorporate them into our lives, but my motto is to "turn every test into a testimony and every mess into a message and every calamity into an opportunity." So write down those messes. Maybe you've experienced several miscarriages. Maybe you've dealt with the loss of your house. Maybe you've been in a serious car accident. Maybe you've been alienated from a certain part of your family.

_____

_____

_____

Okay? I hope this has been helpful already, but let's do a third section.

Let's Talk About Victories!

What have you excelled at—succeeded at—as a grown-up? This may actually take you a little longer to think of because we tend to dwell on our failures and disappointments and pain more than we do on our successes.

We're told, as children, "Don't brag about yourself. Let other people brag about you. Don't be so proud of yourself. That's considered egotistical or boastful or bragging. Be more humble."

The truth is we have quit celebrating ourselves. So let's talk about some major successes that you've had. Let's talk about some minor successes that you've had. Let's talk about things that you have rocked in your world.

Have you lost weight? Have you gotten out of debt? Have you landed a promotion? I don't mean *right now*. I mean what have you done in your life that you're proud of?

- Did you land a part in a play?
- Did you pass your driving test the first time? I didn't. I don't think I've ever admitted that publicly. I failed the first time. I turned into oncoming traffic. So there you go. Now you know my big secret. (I'm sure that state trooper is still in extensive therapy somewhere.)
- Did you come up with an idea that increased the profitability of the company you work for?
- Did you land a big account?
- Did you do something really incredible?
- Did you help somebody find a job?
- Did you "match make" a couple who have a really great marriage?
- Did you pass the bar exam?
- Did you earn your CPA?
- Did you finish high school?
- Did you finish college?

What can we celebrate about you? At one point in our lives, my husband was named employee of the year at his company of five hundred people. That's something he excelled at. I'm really proud of that. I know this is going to be a challenge for some of you because we're not used to celebrating ourselves, but write down five things that you have felt successful at.

_____

_____

_____

_____

_____

Okay? Five. No cheating. Write down five things.

Take a Look Back

Look back at all those sections, and pat yourself on the back and say, "Wow!" Wow! You have survived all that. You have thrived through all that. You are qualified to serve so many people! That is amazing. And I am so proud of you.

Look back at those lists. Using what you've written, let's move on into some business models. Ask the following questions:

- "How could I serve people who want to know about my experience?"
- "How could I teach people how to go through that painful experience?"
- "How could I teach people how to emulate the success that I had?"
- "How could I monetize what makes me smile?"
- "How could I monetize one of those painful experiences so that I can spend more time doing what makes me smile?"

These are key questions. It's a great list. Keep it handy. Now let's talk a little bit about business models.

Drilling Down

What we're going to do is talk a little bit about serving one, serving several, or serving many. I am so passionate about this that I want you to ask yourself in every business model, *Do I want to start serving one-to-one?* That's a way to get to some fast cash immediately.

Or maybe your business is already serving one-to-one and you're looking to increase your profit. So ask: *Am I serving one-to-one, one-to-several, or one-to-many?*

Obviously, the exponential cash will be in serving one-to-many. But sometimes it's just a matter of validating ourselves and getting some of those first sales done.

Look at the model you just chose and think: *Okay, how can I serve more people than I'm already serving?* or *How can I serve the most people in the shortest period of time? Am I going to do ongoing work as a contractor? Am I going to require a retainer?*

Several of the virtual assistants I work with require retainers, meaning I pay them for a minimum of ten hours a month, whether I use five hours or ten hours, and then there's an overage if I go over.

Is it a onetime fee that you're going to charge for something? Are you going to charge for a home-study course and then that's it, or are you going to have a continuity or a membership on the back end?

Are you going to charge per transaction? Maybe you're just going to do some e-books or some books or some CDs, or you're selling widgets in your store, or you're selling flower arrangements. How is that going to look for you?

Let's look at what your revenue models are going to be for those business models too. I don't want you to get too hung up on that yet. I think it's a huge victory that you've gone through your idea prompters and your business models.

Let's just choose a business model that you want to focus on for now, and we can always come back and redo this later when you want to pursue another avenue.

Decide to do it! I am going to give you permission to quit asking around for permission about succeeding in your business.

Quit asking people if what you're doing is a good idea. Quit asking people what they think about this or what they think about that.

Stop caring about what people think. Worry about your market, not your peers. Your peers will change as you grow in business. As you grow and change and move forward, the people you surround yourself with will change, and that can be a little frightening. But I'm giving you permission to pursue this with excellence, with energy, with excitement and enthusiasm. And I want you to know that if you see a need in the market for it, then you can quit looking for reasons why it won't work.

Quit inviting comment. Proceed with confidence. Proceed with excellence and excitement.

I'm so excited for you!

Quit waiting. Quit thinking you need to have every skill. If you don't have the skill, hire the skill. There are so many people who are outsourcing now, affordably. I want you to stop just learning and start earning. You can earn and learn at the same time. Give yourself permission to move forward.

Guess what? This won't be easy. It can be simple, but there will be obstacles. My late friend Jim Thomas would say, "If it was easy, they would call it catchin'—not fishin'—and where would be the fun in that?"

You need to recognize that your obstacles polish you and refine you into the business owner that you need to be.

BAREFOOT ACTION STEP

The Financial Conversation

A wise man should have money in his head, not in his heart.

—Jonathan Swift

**Watch "The Financial Conversation" video
at http://www.barefootexecutivevideos.com/money**

Let's talk about money management a little. I know so many of your situations because I know the situation that I've been in before. I want to tell you that you have got to get a grip on your finances. You have got to pay closer attention.

There are a couple of things that you can do to change your financial situation. We always tend to think, *I just need to make more money.* But until you change your financial habits, making more money doesn't fix anything because you're just going to mismanage that money too.

What you first need to do is evaluate your lifestyle, evaluate your spending. There's a big difference between need and want. My kindergartner came home the other day and said, "We talked about something interesting today in school. We talked about need versus want."

Then she proceeded to tell us at the table what needs were and what wants were, and I think as grown-ups we tend to forget that. We think that a need is an iPhone. I'm going to pick on iPhone users—a need is an iPhone, a need is high-speed Internet, a need is cable with every channel, a need is this brand of shoe or a purse to go with every pair of shoes, or a need is a new car every two years.

The truth is those are wants. Your need is not even to have digital entertainment in your home. If you have an online business you do need the Internet, but some of you could perhaps get away with dial-up or a lower speed, or do like they do in Europe, where they use a lot of Internet cafés because the reliability of their high-speed service at home is not very good.

There are a lot of things that we have classified as needs that really are wants. I don't have any kind of paid television in my house—no cable, no satellite, no anything. I'd rather be investing that money and time into other things.

The fact of the matter is that you really need one pair of dress shoes and one pair of regular shoes—plus maybe a pair of tennis shoes. We could all go months and months without buying any new clothes.

Even your daily Starbucks run or a weekly Starbucks visit or going out to the movies—there are so many places that you can cut your spending. Too many times we cut our spending in the areas of our education, or we cut our spending in the areas of our work skills or our technology tools that really do add to our bottom line.

The fact is, you need to look at some lifestyle things. First, what are some places you and your family can cut spending? Now, second, increase your income. It's hard to increase your income with just a job, you know that. Your boss isn't necessarily going to give you a raise just because you need a raise.

But as a business owner of either a part-time or a full-time business, you are in charge of your income. You're in charge of when you create a new product or offer a new class, or sell more, or present to more people, or make more leads and contacts, or speak more. You are in charge.

As long as you're mismanaging your money on the front end, making more on the back end isn't going to help. I know so many people who have been in debt, severe debt, and paid their way out. They suffered and got out, and guess what? They went right back in debt and then paid their way out again.

It's a cycle. It's much like the weight-loss cycle or the cycle of addictions or habits. You have to address why you have the behaviors that you have before you can fix it. I'm going to challenge you to get a grip on your money management.

Look at your spending. Get out the credit card statements, make a spreadsheet, look at some costs, look at how much cash you're going through, look at how much cash you're not even looking at. Has money ceased to exist? Are you just using plastic and automatic deductions now?

Get a realistic picture on your money and then see where you can cut. I want the very best for you. I know that as you make more and as you get a grip on your finances, you could have more choices and more options and some of those are really fun and sometimes can be really frivolous.

But at the point that you're in stress or conflict or depression or anger over a money situation, that's when you need to wrap your head around what's really going on and how you can best fix it.

BAREFOOT CASE STUDY

Valerie Hayes
Houston, Texas
www.ValerieHayes.com
Pageant Coach

"My success has a lot to do with my ability to quickly diagnose what's holding a contestant back and make easy, fun suggestions on how to improve."

I worked for twenty years as a human resources executive in Fortune 500 companies. I had hit the glass ceiling, and it was difficult to move forward because of my commitments as a wife and mother. Having my own business with a flexible schedule allows me to be a mom, wife, and business professional. I never planned to have my own business because I thought I naturally preferred the security of working for someone else. As it turns out, I love the creativity required to decide how to best meet my clients' needs and love the responsibility of determining my own revenue goals.

At the time I started my business, my children were both in their early to mid-teens, and I needed the flexibility to play chauffeur and attend events related to their various activities. Being in charge of my own workload and schedule enabled me to successfully juggle and have a business that interests me while staying in touch and involved with my family.

The contestants I work with are intelligent, motivated, and goal-oriented young women who use pageant competition as a path for personal development and career networking. In many ways, they're much more interesting and inspiring than the executives I was working with in corporate America.

I doubt three years from now my business will be exactly as it is today. But I enjoy learning, growing, and moving the business in different areas that interest me. I suspect I'll continue as a pageant coach until I'm no longer creatively challenged or inspired by the industry. I don't see that happening for a long time.

My success has a lot to do with my ability to quickly diagnose what's holding a contestant back and make easy, fun suggestions on how to improve. I have an honest, supportive approach that successfully motivates contestants to implement change. I think it's important to speak out about important changes that need to take place in the pageant community. I have developed products and programs to deliver elite-level coaching via the Internet.

I wish I'd seen more clearly when I started my business that no matter what business you're in, you're actually in the business of marketing your business. That's really where all your revenue begins.

PART THREE RECAP

While I'm a firm believer in positive attitude, I don't necessarily believe that "if you believe it, you can achieve it." Some things are simply out of our realm of giftedness, talent, or expertise, Before you *can* achieve anything, however, you must first believe you can. Seems as if I'm contradicting myself, but I'm not.

Consider this: If I don't believe I'll ever be able to dance and I'm convinced I'm a clumsy oaf, then I will never be a functional dancer, much less a great one. If I believe that I can dance, then I follow up with action in the form of lessons and practice, I study with a good teacher, I spend time with other dancers, and I focus on that skill. And I will eventually be a dancer. Maybe not qualified for Radio City Music Hall or *Dancing with the Stars*, but I will be able to dance.

Your business is the same way. You must believe you can work for yourself. You must believe you have skills and gifts and you must believe that this will work even before it does.

Then you get to work with what I call the "Success M&Ms."

Mind-set Keys: Stop comparisons right now! Swim your own race. Stay in your lane. Do your best work. Avoid negativity like a disease.

Massive Action: Quit waiting for your ship to come in. Swim out to meet it. You must know what your motives are and then rank your priorities accordingly. Remember that "hocus pocus, the magic is in the focus" and get to it. You can! Then, commit to a deadline.

Masterminding: Choose a powerful peer group for advancement and accountability. When you invest and throw your money over the bar, your heart tends to follow. Get vested and choose to move forward in a big way.

Mentoring: Save yourself time, money, and heartache by learning from one who has gone before. Choose wisely and intentionally.

Part Four

The Models

Eleven

Service Based:
Use Your Skill Set

*Hide not your talents. They for use were made. What's a
sundial in the shade?*

—Benjamin Franklin

There are several business models. Typically the easiest and lowest-
cost to start with is a service-based business. What do I mean by a
service-based business, and why is it typically the easiest?

How Can You Serve?

Typically, with a service-based business, you can be to cash within a
week, if not two or three days. And that is because you are functioning
with your skill set and what's at your disposal and you're serving other
people in a local or online area.

So let's talk about a service business, just briefly. What do I mean by
a "service business"? Well, maybe you have secretarial skills. So maybe
you have a word-processing service, a typing service, a transcription service, or a virtual-assistant service. Or maybe you outsource yourself to
do a couple of hours of administrative help for people in your local area.

Maybe you hire yourself to go to local offices one day a week. Maybe you're at the chiropractic office Monday, the dentist's office Tuesday, the law office Wednesday, your local church Thursday, and the library Friday, and you are outsourcing your administrative skills for these individuals and businesses. That's a service business.

Other service businesses include lawn care or housecleaning or childcare or hair care or massage therapy or serving people meal preps, like a chef or a meal-delivery service. With accounting, bookkeeping, or working as a handyman—basically, you're exchanging time for money. You're providing a service that people need.

How can you use those discovery questions, exercises, and skill seeking we did a few pages previously to identify a service you could provide and become a service-based business?

My first wildly profitable business was a service-based business. I provided newsletters for people in management in the direct-sales industry—newsletters to motivate their downline, their recruits, and their teams. I typed the newsletters, designed them, provided the material for them, and the clients paid me per month to perform that service for them. Now in my consulting and speaking business, I use several service providers:

- A transcriptionist who types every word (almost) that comes out of my mouth. In Texas, we'd say "Bless her heart."
- A part-time housecleaner
- A person who helps with the yard in the summer (We have seven acres!)
- An accountant who prepares my taxes
- A graphic designer, a Web support person, and an event planner
- A physician, a dentist, a part-time preschool, and other service providers (Sound familiar?)

I didn't start with all this help, but now we've migrated into having a team help with the growth and implementation of our business.

A service-based business is a powerful model and one that almost everyone can implement.

BAREFOOT ACTION STEP

Fishin' Wisdom

The charm of fishing is that it is the pursuit of that which is elusive but attainable, a perpetual series of occasions for hope.

—**John Buchan**

**Watch the "Fishin' Wisdom" video
at http://www.barefootexecutivevideos.com/fishing**

My husband lost his sister when he was a senior in high school. His sister was exactly four years to the day older than he was. Laura and her husband had been married about six months when they had a carbon monoxide leak in their home and died in their sleep.

Eddie was seventeen and the tragedy had a huge impact on him. He and his sister were the only children and his parents were so absorbed in their own grief that Eddie's grief really wasn't acknowledged. They were in survival mode, they were trying to cope, and he was just kind of left to deal with it.

There was a man in his church named Jim. Jim was a crusty older guy who had not had kids and was married to Judy, the love of his life. He was a ceramic tile guy, very much a manual laborer, just as "country" as the day is long. He saw what was going on with this hurting teenage boy and reached out to him.

"You know, every March I go out to the lake and I go fishing; my wife's family has a cabin out there. I really could use a net man, someone to help me bring in the big fish when my hands are full."

Eddie had never been bass fishing; he had done a little dock fishing, but he was not a bass fisherman and there is a lot of skill in that. Anyway, he was really nervous about it, but he was thrilled at the attention and the care that Jim showed him. So Eddie went with him that spring break as a senior in high school. They did that every year for seventeen years.

For seventeen years they fished at the same lake during spring break week and a lot happened in my husband's life during that time. He went off to college (the same college his sister had attended).

But every spring break, fishing was a priority. Jim was very patient with Eddie. He taught him how to cast, what kinds of bait to use, what kinds of rods and reels, how to drive the boat, fishing manners, and even some wise older-man philosophy, and Eddie was a willing student.

Jim really, for lack of a better term, mentored him. Eddie became his fishing apprentice. They had a great time and developed an amazing relationship. Jim and his wife didn't have any children, so Eddie filled that gap for them as well.

At the point Eddie was struggling because his parents were grieving, Jim saw a need and helped fill it. Eddie and Jim became inseparable in so many ways. Even after we met and started dating, one of the tests I had to pass was the "Jim" test. Was Jim going to like me? Was he going to approve of me?

Two thumbs up, I passed big. Jim and I were buddies. We were very close and I really adored him. I adored him mainly for that need he filled in my husband's life. Jim has since gone home to be with the Lord, and spring breaks are a little different now. My husband is still a devout fisherman, however, and now he's teaching our kids.

Jim had this "answer" that I find myself repeating a lot: *"If it was easy they'd call it catchin'—not fishin'—and where would be the fun in that?"*

I repeat that about my business, about my personal goals—I repeat that about so many things. (I've even said it more than once in this book!) Jim inspired us in lots of ways, but a couple of ways in particular.

He taught us that there's opportunity in everyone.

Eddie was just a seventeen-year-old kid who had just lost his sister. Jim didn't have to reach out to him and he sure didn't have to invest seventeen years and spend his fishing vacations with this kid. I tell you what, there is a whole other book about Eddie falling out of the boat, getting hopelessly tangled in weeds, getting lures embedded in his hand, and so many other things Jim had to bail him out of.

Jim didn't have to do all of that, but he did and it changed Eddie's life. I think about that in my business and in my life. Who can I invest in? Who can I be "Jim" for? Who can I take under my wing and mentor? At different stages of our lives and businesses, we need to function in both capacities. Yes, you can be a mentor and also be a mentee.

Jim taught me that you stick with things. If it were easy, where would be the fun in that? There's no sport in that. You just keep trying, you keep wetting your hook, you keep putting the bait out. You do it the right way and you'll have a payday. And even if you don't catch a fish every time, when you're surrounded by the right people and seek out a good "net man," you can still change someone's life.

BAREFOOT CASE STUDY

Traci Knoppe
Missouri
YourWebTechTeam.com
Tech Service Provider, Outsource Services

"I have a team. It's not just me doing the work. I have a team of skilled workers helping me."

I'm a high school graduate, with some college experience, who discovered a knack for all things technical—especially html and Web design. When I encounter a skill or feature request by a client or that I want to learn, I find a tutorial or take a class to learn how to do it. I'm completely self-taught and have been learning for more than a decade and continue to learn in order to to keep my skills up-to-date in the fast-growing, ever-changing Internet world.

I've been online since 1996—when the Internet first came to our city. By 1998, I launched my first successful online business, where I designed my own Web site, set up my own shopping cart system, and connected it to my merchant account. With so many asking me to design their Web sites, I changed my business and launched my Web design company in 1999.

My husband always made a great living, so I only developed my business to the point I wanted to. Then in 2008, we knew my husband would be leaving his employment, and although we thought he would be getting another job, it did not happen. The pressure was on for me to do something to replace his income and to support our family.

So instead of getting a "job" or trying to find a new niche, I changed my business model from a per-hour Web designer to an outsource services company and hired a team to help me. I took action on this idea quickly and was at profit in a mere ten days. I was doing six figures in five and a half months, and our company growth continues.

I love to help people. What I do as a service-based provider is perfect for that, and the fact that I can use my technical skills and knowledge to help someone else grow their business is amazing to me. My clients are successful business owners in their own right; so I truly feel that my services are a team effort and a win-win for everyone to achieve his or her own business success.

I have purposely structured my business to be ongoing. My intention from the beginning was to build a family business that I can one day hand off to my children—so I can retire but the company keeps going. Not all team members are family—but two of my daughters and one son-in-law work for the company, in addition to my husband. It is my hope that one day my three youngest children will also join the company. (I have seven children.)

Shortly after I launched Your Web Tech Team, I decided to run a special sale. It was a low price point, and I gained twenty-one new clients in less than twelve hours! For a service-based business, that's huge. The biggest mistake I made was that I did not really think through what it would look like when that work flowed in. Work piled up. Clients were getting upset. I was in tears and stressed, and while quitting would have been an easy out—and I'll admit I thought about it—I knew I had to find a way to make it work, as this was our only income.

Ineffectiveness, poor work habits, exaggerated capabilities of new team members, and my own lack of thinking through my price points nearly drove my business into the ground.

Several clients left. I ultimately realized I needed to change who my target market was and adjust my pricing accordingly. During the transition to that new market, I let go all my former team and started over after I started gaining the new target clients.

So I changed direction, kept going, and am now doing better than ever. All because I did not quit when things got rough. I found a way to make it work.

Twelve

Expertise Based: Coaching and Consulting

Success is the maximum utilization of the ability that you have.

—Zig Ziglar

Can You Share Your Experience?

In addition to the service model, there's also the coaching and consulting model. What experience do you have? Go back to your experience exercises on previous pages. What experience do you have that you can teach other people?

One of my clients is attorney Dan Scott, who has been practicing law for twenty-five years. Very successful, very profitable, Dan has a heart of gold. And at this stage of his life, he also has the desire to be traveling and doing mission work, so he needs not to be as tied to his office.

We have now created an additional business income stream for him where he mentors and consults with young attorneys. When they get out of law school, they may know how to practice law, but they don't know how to run a business. They don't teach you that in law school, evidently. So Dan is mentoring young attorneys in how to have a profitable practice. He's doing that through technology, teleclasses, and webinars; he's also doing some in-person weekend events.

Find out who you are and do it on purpose.
—Dolly Parton

Perhaps coaching and consulting are ways that you can turn your experience into cash flow. I do business consulting and strategizing; there are life coaches and health and nutrition coaches. How could you implement that as a business model?

There is an entire industry based on the coaching model:

- nutrition coaches
- life coaches
- style coaches
- weight-loss coaches
- spirituality coaches
- business coaches (in every niche imaginable)
- productivity coaches

You name it—there is a coach for it. While I don't believe you have to be certified as a coach, I do believe you need to choose your coach carefully when you are hiring and that you need to be careful about calling yourself a coach unless you have some great experience and some clients behind you. Don't slap "coach" on your name and start charging. Do a little research into the industry. Seek out the "best practices" for coaching and see where a good fit for you falls.

I consider consulting a different model than coaching. Consultants take their specific expertise and go into an organization, business, or institution to diagnose and remedy a certain problem or project. Again, these take many shapes, but I know there are:

- leadership consultants
- sales consultants

- software consultants
- team dynamic consultants
- downsizing consultants, and more

How could your specific skill set or expertise transform into a freelance consulting operation? Companies are trending to hire consultants because of the specialized expertise available, the ability to not commit to a hiring situation, and the benefits of no commitment to the long term. Alan Weiss is an expert at transforming your life into that of a consultant, and I highly recommend his books on pricing and positioning.

No matter what model you choose, you'll always come back to a common objection: "But I'm just me—why would they listen to me?"

Ears, Eyes, and Fingertips:
The Power of Being *You*!

Let's talk a little bit about relationship marketing and personality marketing. There are many ways to integrate personality and the calendar and fun promotions into what you're doing.

As I've mentioned before, people can copy what you're teaching, but even if they try to copy you word-for-word, they can't be you. Nobody else can be me, so I don't get too stressed about somebody taking my audience by being me.

I'm uniquely me, with my own fingerprints, with my own accent, with my own experience. And I want you to embrace that about you. I want you to put a lot more *you* into your business.

Here are several of my favorite ways to do this—and I'll just skim these really quickly.

Video

Simple video is my favorite way. I use it a lot. I use my easy little Flip camera. I use video, and lots of examples of how I use video can be found at YouTubeBarefoot.com and BarefootExecutive.TV.

Video is very powerful. That way you see my eyes; you see my expressions. You know how I'm tilting my head, and you know how passionate

I am about what I'm talking about. Video is very powerful and it can be very inexpensive.

I have a lot of videos, and that's why you may feel as if you know me already, because you've seen me on video. Video is a very powerful way to inject more of you into what you're doing.

Audio

Audio, to me, is less preferable than video. But some of you are just not going to get in front of a camera. I understand that. Audio is fast, it's easy, and it's you. It's something you can strip to an mp3 player, rip to a CD, or listen to online.

It doesn't have to be expensive. You can use Audacity from Sound Forge, Audio Acrobat, or even a conference line like FreeConferenceCall.com.

You can record with a phone or directly into your computer without any fancy mic setup. Audio is also a very powerful way to get more of you into your marketing, even if you just put up a photo of you with an audio underneath it. That helps increase your conversions from prospects to clients. That helps your audience "reach out and touch you."

Current Photos

I would inject more of you into your marketing and into your business with photography—simple photos, snapshots, a professional headshot. Now, that being said, a freelance photographer took my professional headshot in my backyard. Or you can just pick a quality snapshot that you like.

But I do caution you to make sure it's current and that it's not too "airbrushed" or too perfect because when people meet you in person or see your videos, you don't want there to be a huge disconnect.

Write in Your Own Voice

I want you to write with your sense of humor. I want you to write stories about you. The power of story is phenomenal. Nothing can take its place. You'll notice I use the power of story a lot.

When you have videos, audios, photos, stories, and then use social media such as Facebook, Twitter, YouTube, and LinkedIn to circulate your content and your conversations to several different affinity groups—that is the magic formula. Those things will wrap up so much of you that you have to be authentic, you have to be transparent, and people will have no doubt who they're dealing with when they're doing business with you.

BAREFOOT ACTION STEP

The Charm of Little Brothers

Giving frees us from the familiar territory of our own needs by opening our mind to the unexplained worlds occupied by the needs of others.
—Barbara Bush

Watch "The Charm of Little Brothers . . ." video at http://www.barefootexecutivevideos.com/brothers

I have three brothers; two are older, and we call the older three of us the "original set" because we pretty much grew up together. And as the baby of the family I was supposed to be the last one, but when I was seventeen my parents adopted again and we suddenly had a baby boy in the house.

So I now have a little brother who is in his early twenties and I call him my "first kid" because he was my first really close experience with a baby, and we are very, very close. I adore him. He helped me delay my own decision to have children for several years.

Anyway, he's a typical twentysomething; he's figuring school out and trying to decide what he wants to do as a grown-up and making all those kinds of decisions you make at that age. What I've noticed is that he is very helpful, very attentive, and very family connected when he needs something.

For instance, last week I started getting some random texts checking on me, seeing how I was doing and checking on the kids, so I was waiting for it. Sure enough, I was out of town and got a text asking if I needed anything done around the house, any yard work done, or anything done on the cars.

I was guessing that his insurance was due, and like many young adults, he's not very good at budgeting yet, so he needed some cash. He knows better than to ask for money outright, he knows I don't play that way, and he knows that I don't give handouts even to my own kids, so he asked how he could be of service because he needed something.

I love my brother and I love to help him out and I love to receive a service in return, but I do have to admit that I would like to hear from him more often. I would like it if he were more interactive and involved at other times even when he didn't need something. That would go a long, long way with his big sister.

I think probably your clients, your prospects, and your customers are the same way. I think they would like to hear from you at times when you're not promoting something or in launch mode or serving them. I think they would like to hear, "How are you doing?" or "Here's some content I thought you would like" or "Oh, look at this interesting fact" or just you sharing stories.

Not to say that when you contact them there can't be an offer in the resource guide or in the pdfs or whatever, but they know the difference when you only show up around money time, when you only show up when you have something going on and you need to pay the bills. They recognize it on social media, they recognize it in e-mail marketing, and they recognize it in direct mail. They have their radar up just as I do with my little brother.

I'm going to encourage you to stay in touch with your family, your clients, and your prospects. Stay in touch with them even when you don't have anything to directly benefit from them, knowing that the miles in that relationship will go really far if you nurture it.

I still love my brother and I love to give him the opportunity to help, and your customers probably love you and the things that you offer them, but they'll be even happier if you stay connected without a motive.

BAREFOOT CASE STUDY 1

Ann Vertel
San Diego
http://AnnVertel.com
Entrepreneur Mind-set Expert

"I get to create new things every day and creators don't retire—I'll probably be doing this till my dying day."

As an entrepreneur mind-set and success psychology expert, I help entrepreneurs create a business and a life of excellence. I started off in one of the most rigid organizations in the world—the military—and both my parents were naval officers, so I guess it was in my blood. My educational background is psychology. That, coupled with years of experience teaching leadership to mid-grade and senior officers, led me to seek a second career that was profoundly rewarding and built on my skills. My mantra became, "My rules. My hours. My dress code."

After a successful twenty-year career as a naval officer, I wanted to be home for my family. Transitioning from a full-time military person to a full-time entrepreneur didn't actually seem like such a challenge; I think I'd always been a rebel in a uniform anyway, and now I get to make my own rules.

In my work it is an absolute thrill to see people who thought they were limited by the constraints or rules of others taking bold steps toward fulfilling their dreams. I get to create new things every day—and creators don't retire.

I have quality time with my daughter before school, a run on the beach or a workout at the gym, then a few hours of writing, filming, or connecting on social media. Once my family gets home, I'm all theirs!

Working for myself, I use my creativity, stretch my boundaries, and am not limited by others. The money I make is based on the value I bring to the market and not by just trading my time for money. And I define what my life looks like and how work fits into my life, not the other way around.

A few years back my server crashed and I lost everything. It took months to regain my traction, and it was hard to build momentum. Even through that, I never really thought about quitting—what else could possibly be more interesting than creating your own life's work?

BAREFOOT CASE STUDY 2

Melissa Ingold
Ontario, Canada
YourIMSweetie.com
http://www.internetmarketingsweetie.com
Online Marketing Training

"Forget about clamoring and clawing your way to get ahead of your competitor—unless you're prepared for a quick crash and burn."

I was a high school dropout, pregnant at nineteen. I didn't have an education, just a love of writing. So I started writing. When my daughter turned a year old, I moved to a small town and rented a little house of my own. I fired up my computer with a determination to make my daughter's life better. I was a young, single mother on welfare, with no education and no prospects, but I had a fire inside of me that I can't really explain. I also had a vision of what I wanted my life to be like. There was no way I was going to spend the rest of my life scrounging to pay bills and just survive. A few months after I moved to my new town, I met my husband.

Through all of that I was using the Internet to research a way to make money. I tried a lot of business opportunities. I wasted a lot of money I didn't have. I was frustrated beyond belief because I wasn't making any money, but I had all these info products on my computer that were supposed to be the "sure thing." But then a lightbulb went off. Why not do what I was good at? I mean, I was an okay writer, and I knew there were a ton of opportunities to be found online. So that's what I did.

Before I knew it, people were paying me to write material for their Web sites. Not long after my son was born, I decided to enroll in a program at the local library that would allow me to finish the four credits I needed to graduate from high school. It was mandatory that I complete grade 12 English, but I had options for the other three courses, so I chose three different computer courses. I figured the computer courses would be really easy, but I had no idea they would be the start of something amazing.

When my writing shifted from content writing to copy writing, that was really the turning point for me. I discovered I had a knack for it, and before I knew it, I was booked two to three months in advance as a copywriter. I was making good money, but I was burnt out from all the work.

That led me to start my first membership site out of a need to create passive income so that I could get out of the service business. The following year I landed a big client that required me to pull together a team of people to work with me. I became the project manager, worked directly with my clients, and outsourced the work to my team.

My membership site was growing. My affiliate income was growing. My business was growing in a big, big way. It was also the year I gave birth to my second son.

Our third child was diagnosed with Gaucher's disease and when he was a few months old, I spent two weeks in the hospital with him so he could have every test imaginable.

Looking back, I'm very thankful that I had my own business so that I could take care of my special-needs baby. I wouldn't have been able to work at a regular job, and it would have made our lives even more stressful in regards to time, energy, and especially finances.

Fairly quickly, my passive income far exceeded what I was making from client projects, so I closed down my service business. I wasn't an overnight success by any means. I've worked hard, struggled, and made a lot of sacrifices to get to this point. But looking back, I'm glad I didn't throw in the towel.

It's not impossible. It's not just a pipe dream. But there are no short-cuts either, no easy ways to the top—I mean, it took me ten years from the day I decided to work from home to get to today, to multiple six figures. You put in the work—you get results.

I focus on helping people use integrity-driven marketing methods, because one of the most valuable assets as a business owner is your reputation. I want to provide them with an alternative to all the get-rich-quick, cutthroat, and sometimes unethical Internet marketing information available online today. I want to help them create the best business they can.

This is something I see myself doing forever. I can see myself sharing my business with my kids and even grandkids. One of the things that I am working toward is eventually creating a foundation in my son's name to raise money for families with Gaucher's Disease Type 2/3, and for research. I want to help the families financially because there are so many expenses, and one parent needs to be at home taking care of the child.

Thirteen

Knowledge Based: Information Marketing

*My life—my personality, my habits, even my speech—
is a combination of the books I choose to read, the
people I choose to listen to, and the thoughts I choose
to tolerate in my mind.*

—Andy Andrews

What Do You Know?

Let's talk about the information model. We have talked about the service model and the expertise model. Later we will talk about the product-driven model, like the e-commerce or the store-driven model.

But what about *information*? What does that mean? It means turning your brain into something you can take to the bank. You can take your brain to the bank by creating information products: audios, videos, how-to products, self-help products.

Capture more of yourself using technology and turn that into products you can sell—online or after a speaking event or in person. The information model will help you take your experience, your skill set, the painful things you've overcome, and the things you feel successful about and turn those into a market.

For instance, I have a client who's lost 175 pounds, and now she is coaching and mentoring and creating products so that other people can also discover their bones. And I love her market and how she's turned her experience into something to share on a much more global level.

I was an individual business owner working at home, and now I work with at-home professionals, counseling them, strategizing with them, consulting with them, and training them how to do the same thing that I did.

How can Dan Scott, the Tennessee attorney I mentioned in the previous chapter, create products? He can do audios and checklists and worksheets and guidelines and blueprints on how to build a successful business as an attorney. And you can do the same with your market or your expertise, so I want you to think about that too.

Some of these models are time-for-money, some are products-for-money, and some can be more passive because of other ways you can build income. With the information product, for instance, you create the product once—much the same as I'm doing with this book, my CDs, and my DVDs—and it sells over and over again through your online business, your offline business, or through a bookstore. When you speak, you could take products with you too.

Let me tell you first the benefits of info marketing—why I believe you should do info marketing: It's invaluable. It's immediate. It's inexpensive. It's in demand.

You say, "Wait, wait, wait, Carrie. Those are all the same reasons you gave us for starting a service business."

And? If it's invaluable, immediate, inexpensive, and in demand, then there's another stream of income, which is what this book is all about. That is a benefit of info marketing.

Maybe you've been racking your brain for a service business or a membership business or a coaching business, and maybe none of that resonated with you. Maybe info marketing will.

What Is an Information Product?

Info marketing means you're selling "information products"—so what is an information product?

Your only experience in this area might be "how to make money" products or "how to have an online business" products or the "how to scam" stuff. Don't dismiss it because of those.

Let me just say that there are info products in every niche or market out there. Adoption, weight loss, fertility, marriage, relationships, dating, how to pick up women, how to pick up men, how to have your kids be better behaved, how to garden, how to garden in pots, how to be a healthier cook, how to be a vegetarian cook, how to be a raw chef—

You can do info products on all those subjects, so I don't want you to think that info marketing has to do with only one niche. Info marketing, like every other model that I've taught you, is a model in which you can put any market or niche. I want you to sweep those cobwebs out of your brain and uncross your arms, and I'm going to tell you what info products are.

Info products are audios, books, classes, downloads, electronic tools, and software.

You can go through the whole alphabet. You can do articles, you can do videos—which you know is one of my favorites—you can do webinars. You can think of all kinds of info products.

Info products simply mean information you are sharing in a form that customers can purchase from you. Think about that. You're giving them information and they're giving you money. It's not selling air—it's selling information.

"Oh, but Carrie, I don't know if I want to be in that kind of business."

I know people who think this way. They really think there's some hocus pocus going on, that we're pulling the wool over people's eyes. I think they say we are "selling air."

Let me just talk to you about some well-known info marketers. Who was your first grade teacher? What was her name? Do you see her in your mind? She was an info marketer. Your parents paid her to swap her information with you. She didn't give you anything tangible. She shared the information that she had so that you would be better equipped to go serve with your gifts, right?

What about a librarian? What about any published author? You don't hear people griping about spending money on a book at the bookstore. That's information marketing. It's just in a very tangible, physical form.

Perhaps you paid for college. You paid for a degree. You paid for welding school. You paid for acting classes, piano lessons, voice lessons—you're paying those teachers for the information in their brains.

What's in Your Brain?

So why not take the information in your brain to the bank? Just because we're delivering it with technology and the media with the Internet, why all of a sudden do we have some kind of stigma associated with it?

I'm a certified teacher for pre-K through 12. I also could teach some college classes in different subjects. Why does that kind of info marketing hold any higher weight than online info marketing? It makes no sense to me why we put up these silly roadblocks and negative connotations when there is really no *new* idea—just a different evolution of ideas using different technology or forms of payment.

If what I know is valuable to someone else, I can exchange that for money—I am an information marketer, just like your piano teacher, Mrs. Steen; just like your second grade teacher, Miss Hewitt; just like Dr. White, your college professor. They were information marketers. I want you to get over any stigma you may attach to information marketing.

Instead of standing at the front of a college class or teaching in the public school system, we're going to leverage technology for this. We're going to put this in audios, webinars, and books (whether they're electronic or physical or manuals or worksheets or tools).

Classes are also one of my favorite ways to do this because the information immediate. You have the live energy of an audience; you are creating as you go; and there is no editing, overanalyzing, and endless tweaking before you decide to sell it. You sell it based on the concept of the material and then deliver it "on demand."

E-reports, checklists, diagrams, spreadsheets—they all become info products. Remember the Time-Life book series my dad subscribed to? Yup—info product!

The book you are holding in your hand is an information product. I will also record an audio and several supplemental videos. Selling information products means that I am an information marketer. If that is our definition, then Zig Ziglar, John C. Maxwell, Dave Ramsey, Robin McGraw, and even Julia Child are information marketers. Wow! Really? Yes! Really.

Info marketing is serving one-to-many at its very best. I have products that I've sold to hundreds and hundreds of people whom I've never met, and I have coaching programs and webinars and boot camps that have served people whom I've never met—one-to-many.

I can teach seventy to seven thousand people through technology at one time, and I don't have to leave my house and I don't have to necessarily get a babysitter. And I don't have to apply for a job to see if the college or the community center or the school thinks I'm worthy. I know I can take my skill set and exchange money for that.

Why Is It Invaluable?

We've said it's invaluable, first of all, because it's uniquely you. We've talked before about the fact that you don't think you're qualified enough and you don't think you're expert enough. I hope we don't have to go over all that again. I hope you believe me by now that you are incredible! You're marvelous and you are specially equipped to teach what you know from your experience, your skill set, and so forth. It's uniquely you. It's your story.

By now you know my story, how I have overcome extreme obesity, extreme debt, infertility, depression, self-confidence issues, and on and on. I've even overcome some business failures, and I have some strategies and tools in place now that I've overcome those things. That's part of my story.

The other part of my story is that I'm the mom of four beautiful children, true gifts from God, and I am a wife, and I'm in Texas, and I work at home. That's why I'm called the Barefoot Executive, because I work at home on my terms. I don't dress for anybody else, I don't have anybody else's schedule, and I deal with my life on my terms.

My husband and I were having coffee this morning at breakfast, and we were getting the baby ready to take her to story time because Wednesday is our date together. She and I head to the local public library (remember those?) just to hang out.

My husband works with our company full-time. He's our CFO, the chief of all things financial, because I am not so good with numbers. I tell him, "I'll make the money, you manage it, and that way everybody will be happy."

He looked at me over his coffee and repeated what he tells me often, "Carrie, we have an extraordinary life and I'm so proud of what you do and how you're so passionate about changing the world one business owner at a time."

That to me is being the Barefoot Executive. That is worth a whole lot of heartache and frustration and obstacles and wrestling the alligators that I sometimes wrestle.

Your story is uniquely you. What have you overcome? What have you experienced? What are you equipped to do? Nobody else has the same skill set you do. Maybe they've been trained the same way as you, but they do it differently than you.

If you don't believe me, I like this tip that I got from another work-at-home professional, Rhea Perry, who also home educates her children. Rhea said, "Anytime you have a writer's block or an experience block, go to Google and look up some articles on your area of expertise, interest, market, or service. Read what your competition is writing, and then you say, 'I could do better than that!' or 'I totally disagree with that' or 'Here's how I would do that differently' or 'I think I might try it this way.'"

That's when you know you have experience or knowledge or a unique skill set in that area. So I challenge you to test your experience level and your style. Nobody else has the style that you do.

Are there other people in the work-at-home professional market like me? Absolutely. Are there other people in the online marketing space? Yes, there absolutely are. What about other people in the mom space or the woman space or the fill-in-the-blank space? Yes, yes, yes. There are several crowded markets.

Do they scare me? No, because I can be imitated and emulated but I will never be duplicated. I'm uniquely me, and I want you to remember that about you. You are uniquely you.

I want you to embrace the *you* that you were created to be. Quit worrying about competition. Quit worrying about somebody taking your idea or taking your intellectual property.

You know what? Take my intellectual property. I can make more. I can create more reports and write more things because you can't write the way that I would write. You can't tell the same stories about Baby Barefoot that I can. You haven't adopted two children and given birth to two children while losing one hundred pounds and coming out of $100,000 worth of debt. You haven't done that the way I've done that.

But guess what? You've done a lot of things that I haven't done in a way that I haven't done them. So you be you and don't be worried about what someone else has done.

I'm not saying don't think of your market or your niche or your unique thing. I'm not telling you to say, "Oh, that works for Carrie. I'm going to go in and do that exactly like her." I'm telling you to be you with your story, your skill set, and your style. I think there's plenty of room for all of us.

I don't get too worked up about competition. I don't get too worked up about other people in the space because I think if I'm not serving my customers or my audience the way they need to be served—if they choose to be on somebody else's list or attend somebody else's class, then more power to them. I want them to be served in the way that they need to be served.

I want you to get comfortable with that in your market and with your information. That's why your information product will be invaluable.

Why Is It Immediate?

It is superfast to create an information product. How long does it take me to create a one-hour webinar? It takes about an hour. I have to do some prep time, I have to do some set-up with my technology team, but for the most part you can create an audio, a video, an article, a book— you can create that superfast because it goes from "here to creation," and we'll talk a little bit about that in a minute.

How fast can it be? Well, can you talk? Clearly you can talk. Can you type? I think you probably can. Can you teach what you know?

My seven-year-old can teach my four-year-old several things. My fifteen-year-old can teach my fourteen-year-old several things. And guess what? My teenagers can teach me several things.

What Can You Teach?

Can you teach? Absolutely. You can teach what you know, and again you're going to use your skill set, your style, and your story to do it.

If you think you have this obstacle—or that obstacle—or maybe your vision is a problem or arthritis in your hands is a problem, and you're going to give me a list of excuses, then let me tell you about my friend Matt, who's also an information marketer.

Matt makes more than $50,000 a month in his information marketing business, and Matt is completely blind.

Let me tell you about Rhonda, the Story Lady, who's an information marketer online. She's also blind, and every time I see Rhonda at a conference she has her guide dog with her.

Marcia is my scrapbook lady. She keeps the Barefoot family scrapbooks up-to-date. Marcia has multiple sclerosis and cannot work outside of her home on a consistent basis. She could feel sorry for herself, apply for aid, and be dependent on others the rest of her life, but she chooses to use her skill set, her space, and her software to be a can-do kind of gal. I love that! And I believe that for you too—no matter your circumstance, gender, or skill level.

So I don't want you to start giving me obstacles or excuses about why you can't be an information marketer. "Carrie, I'm mute. I don't have a voice. I can't do audio recordings." Then maybe you can type or maybe you can write it out and someone else can transcribe it for you.

You can find voice-over specialists on Craigslist or on Twitter or Facebook who will put a voice to what you're writing. So please, don't let those things stop you. More than ever before there is no reason that you can't succeed at this type of marketing.

It's immediate—superfast—to create. As a matter of fact, my friend Paul Evans will tell me he'll wake up with an idea and before noon he has a new product. It can be that fast.

Why Is It Inexpensive?

Information marketing can be very inexpensive as a business. You can use trial offers or use free conference call lines. Instant Teleseminar has a trial. You can use PayPal and ClickBank to start your accounts. Those are low- and no-cost strategies.

I started my business when I was very much in debt, so I know what it's like to do business on a shoestring. Yes, I have a little more freedom now when I'm developing things, but when I first started I was watching every penny and then some. It was important for me to be profitable very quickly.

Even now when I create a product or launch something or come out with a new class, I know exactly what it's costing me to produce it, and I know exactly when I'm at the break-even point. I know, for instance, if I have to do two sales or ten sales before I get to profit. It's very important to me to not dig deeper in debt and to not be functioning at a red level all the time. Some products I do develop at a cost to myself before I sell them. A lot of times I like to presell so that I'm covering my cost and my expenses before I even start.

A Flip camera is one of my absolute favorite things. It uses AA batteries. That and a YouTube account can get you up and running and building an audience quickly. No editing or fancy equipment required!

My point is that if you have access to any of these things—telephone recordings, video recordings, a Flip camera, Audio Acrobat, free pdf converters, or GoToWebinar—you can create many products. You can create audios, books, classes, downloads, electronic tools, software, and so forth. It doesn't have to cost you a lot.

"But Carrie, what about merchant accounts and what about fancy software?"

You don't need them. Willie Crawford told me recently how he created his first soul food cookbook. He started with a free blog and by gathering names with a squeeze page. He created his soul food cookbook as a Word document. He typed it up himself and took it to the local copy shop to fulfill orders. He makes $300,000 a year because of that cookbook, the leads it generated, and other products and services with the list that he built using Word. He didn't even convert it to pdf format at first, but simply used Word and then printed it out.

You can use any kind of free pdf converter. My Mac has a pdf converter built into the printer spool. You don't need Adobe Professional unless you need to alter pdf documents, so don't invest in that product, at least not yet. You really can build on a shoestring. Look at me! You really can.

And I honestly prefer that. More money does not make it better. I would rather you invest in coaching and masterminding and skill sets than in developing any of these products.

As far as merchant accounts and things, PayPal and ClickBank are fine to start with. I know that Craig Ballantyne of Turbulence Training and Jimmy D. Brown of IM Institute do high six and seven figures with these tools. If it's good enough for them, I think it's good enough for us too. You can check out my resources page at Barefoot-Executive.com for more suggestions.

Why Is It in Demand?

People are searching for answers related to the same things that you already know. Google and search engines prove this. The fact is, we're in an information age and folks are searching for answers and we are the ones who provide them. It's the ultimate crowd-sourcing. Your information products are in demand. People want to know what you know. It's in demand.

But What Do I Know?

What do people frequently ask you to help them solve? What do you get phone calls about from your family and friends? What kinds of questions do you find yourself answering over and over? What knowledge do you feel a little bit superior about? What's a really tough experience you've gone through successfully? What's something you feel you should write a book about?

People want to know what you know. If you don't believe me, go to Amazon.com and type in a couple of words about your interest. Type in a couple of words about your market and your expertise and see if other people have written books that apply to your area of expertise and interest. See if other people bought those books.

Do a little research. Go to Google and see what kind of results come up. Go to www.search.twitter.com and see if people are talking about what you know. Go to Facebook and see if there are groups developed around it or if there are threads or people talking about it. People want to know what you know.

We're really bad about overvaluing everyone else and undervaluing ourselves. We tend to compare everyone else's strengths to our weaknesses. I want you to quit undervaluing yourself. You are a rock star in several areas, and you need to tap into those.

I could become an information marketer in one of many areas. We talked about weight loss and debt, infertility, adoption, depression. I was a military kid. I was a ministry kid. I'm a musician. I went to six different colleges in four years and never dropped a credit hour. I could create an information product based on that.

I paid off debt at a record pace without bankruptcy or consolidation loans, and I repaired my credit at lightning-fast speed. I could create an information product about that.

I could create information products about esteem for women or raising kids with an age gap. I could create a product on raising my special-needs child.

I could create an information product about being a businesswoman in a sea of businessmen. I could create a product on having a virtual office because I've had a virtual office for nine years, before virtual was cool. There are so many things that I could create an information product about.

I hope you just said: "Well, if she could write information products about that, I could do this!"

- Have you recovered from a surgery?
- Have you survived cancer?
- Have you had any kind of physical therapy?
- Have you had a near-death experience?
- Have you come back from a hardship of any kind?
- Have you raised a difficult child?
- Have you transformed the behavior of one of your children?
- Have you come out of an abusive situation?
- Have you conquered a perilous situation of debt?

- Have you overcome a job loss? Have you been fired? Have you been downsized?
- Have you entered a new career field in midlife?
- Have you been able to invest money in a way that people said would fail, but it worked?

What have you done that you could share with other people? Maybe it's just learning a new skill set at a different age. My dad was the first high school graduate in his family, period—not just among his brothers and sisters, I mean in his family. Not only that, he was the first one in his family who went into the military and became career military. The rest of them just went in for a tour or two and then left. My dad spent twenty-seven years in the United States Coast Guard and was the highest-ranking enlisted officer possible.

Then my dad retired and went to college. He was the first college attendee, much less graduate, in his family, and he attended in midlife with three teenagers. He could also teach you contracting, which he learned from those now-famous remodeling books. I'm superproud of my dad. My dad could write an information product on several things.

He could teach you how to implement PowerPoint with multimedia. He's seventy-two years old and he learned PowerPoint from information products and can teach it too—information technology for seniors, technology for ministers—he could do so many of those things. He could teach you how to raise support for something you're passionate about. He could teach you event planning, speech preparation, and team mobilization in times of crisis. He could teach you disaster recovery and water safety and—well, I think you get the point.

My dad has a wealth of experience, and I would venture to say that no matter your age, no matter what you feel that your lack or your experience is, you've got something other people want to know.

I want to challenge you to go to Amazon, Google, Twitter, or Facebook and see who's talking about it, who's looking for it, and how you can benefit them.

"Okay, Carrie, I'm a believer! I know I can be an information marketer too. What do I do first?"

How Can You Find Your Market?

First you define your market. Now let me back up a little and say that my friend Paul and I were having a conversation the other day.

He said, "You know, online businesspeople are the only business-people who say, 'Okay, I don't know anything about business and I don't know anything about my market and I don't know anything about this, but I've heard that strength training is hot and it's searched for, so I want to develop a product on that. So first teach me strength training, and then teach me how to create a product about it.'

"Whereas somebody offline is going to say, 'You know what, I'm a really great baker. I can make pie like nobody's business. I'm going to open up a bakery, but I just don't have the business skill set. So I'll bring my experience to the table, and you just help me with the business.' "

I'm a business coach. I'm a strategist—that's what I do, so I can't teach you what you know. You have to bring what you know to the table, so quit trying to come up with something new that you think is hot or trendy. Come up with what you know. It will make your journey that much easier and your road to profits that much faster.

Define your market. In the case of the pie baker, the market is people who love pies or people who are too busy to make their own pies or people who are entertaining and need pies.

Define your market.

- Whom will you market to?
- What do they want in a product?
- What can you create simply?

We'll go into more detail on these in just a minute. Are you with me? I'll help you with the details.

Whom will you market to? Do you have a list or an audience who will listen to you?

Social Media

Do you have followers on Twitter, Facebook, YouTube, or LinkedIn?

Do you have an e-mail list? If you don't, you absolutely must begin ethically collecting e-mails for a targeted group of prospects and clients.

Do you have a permission-based e-mail list? Even if you only have a few hundred, that's a start. You've seen the fishbowl drawings in restaurants, tanning salons, florists, and local businesses? Those folks should be collecting e-mail addresses! There is rarely a purchase I make at the mall or some local spot where I'm not asked my zip code, my phone, and my e-mail addresses. These are smart marketers and they want to follow up with specials, incentives, customer appreciation days, and traffic-driving behaviors to get more eyes, ears, and wallets into their storefront, either virtual or physical.

If you don't have a social media list or a permission-based e-mail list, what about affiliate partners or collaborators? Whom do you know who might be a competing market or service? You can go through affiliate marketing. For instance, if you come to me and you have a really great product but you don't have an audience and your product seems like a good match for mine, if it fits into my promotional calendar and I think it's something to which my audience would respond well, I could promote your product for a commission.

Paid Advertising

To test a market, you could always go to Google and use "pay per click" advertising to drive targeted traffic to your information or sales page. You could pay for placement in someone else's newsletter in an overlapping industry. Say you develop a product on a detoxification diet or holistic healing methods. You might approach SelfGrowth.com and place a paid solo mailing or sponsored ad in their alternative health newsletter. They already have the list and the "vehicle" and you could leverage it, if you have the funds that will get folks to your list and your offer.

There are many newsletters, blogs, and places online and offline where you can do some integrative placement and get your news, information, and list-builder in front of the right targeted traffic.

So do you have a list or an audience? This is your market. What do they want? What does your market want? If you have a list or an audience, or even social media—that's something you can get up and running very quickly, a social media audience.

If you have a list or an audience, ask them what they want. Ask them! Use www.SurveyMonkey.com and see what they need, where their gaps are, what they want to know from you. You can get up to one hundred responses and it's free—that's a really great tool.

Monitor Your Competition

You can also monitor your competition. Remember I said don't get too worked up about competition. But use them for market research and for what you feel are deficits in the market.

Go to ClickBank. I love this. Vonalda, one of my clients, said recently, "I went to ClickBank to look at some other things that are out there, and I was just disgusted at what was out there, and they're selling!" She went to see what people are looking for. That product wouldn't be there if nobody was buying it, so look at what they're doing and decide how you can do it better.

You might get on others' e-mail lists and see what kinds of things they're marketing or selling to their lists.

Affiliate Promote

Here's another way that I like to test ideas for products or services before putting any money or time or energy into a product or service. Even though it's cheap and easy to produce these, it does take some energy. So before you do that, you might affiliate promote some things to your list.

Before I came up with a product on getting multiple streams of income, I might host a free call with my list to see who's interested in learning about multiple streams of income. I might ask, "Do you think this is a viable product or service that I can offer—teaching multiple streams of income?" I had fifteen hundred folks register for a series that I did on that very topic. You see how that works?

But you can affiliate promote something, too, and then if your list is responsive to that, you might want to pursue that road. If your list did not respond at all, then either it wasn't a good offer for your list or your list is not interested. It may just be that your list didn't respond to that person's offer or energy, so you do have to kind of use your gut level on some of that.

Developing Your Product or Service

Developing a product or service is not about what you want to create. It's not about what you think people need or what you're in love with or you're passionate about. It's about what your market wants to spend money on. It's about solving a problem for them, not about getting the book out of your head that you feel you need to get out of your head.

It's not like, "Oh, but this would change so many lives!" Well, it could if they want it, if they want to change their life that way, so get over what you love and what you want to do, and first find a way to merge what your audience wants with what you can provide. That is a huge key. Do not get so in love with your idea that you forsake all reason.

Milana Leshinksy of Coaching Millions said to me, "Sell them the dessert and then give them their vegetables as a bonus. No one wants to buy the vegetables."

Keeping that in mind, what can you create quickly? Articles, e-books, how-to guides?

I consulted with somebody who's been blogging for more than a year. I asked, "How often have you been blogging? How many blog posts do you have?" She had one hundred blog posts. That's a book, that's a course, that's a series. Joanne's market is grief recovery, and her *Heartache to Healing* blog is providing the content for her material, much like Willie Crawford's soul food blog provided the material for his cookbook. (Is this starting to click with you now?)

How can you create something quickly? You can repurpose articles. You can write an e-book quickly. It doesn't have to be perfect; it just has to be done.

You can do interviews. That's one of my favorites, leveraging other people's expertise and talent with interviews. Again, go back to FreeConferenceCall.com or AudioAcrobat.com or InstantTeleseminar.com and do interviews. You can create products that way. Have them transcribed and then you have a written product too.

You could do a solo audio with AudioAcrobat.com or a little Olympus recorder. I carry mine almost everywhere. You can create solo audios of you teaching. This week, I'm writing while I'm on a cruise ship with my

139

family. After I work on my manuscript for a bit, I'm also going to use Audacity (a free software program) on my laptop and record a class for one of my group mentoring programs. I can literally create anywhere—even in the middle of the ocean!

You could do a video series like I do at www.BarefootVideoCoach.com or www.MagneticListBuilding.com. I also have twenty-five videos that go with *25 Tips for Keeping Your Funnel Full*. I've only released it in report form so far, but I have twenty-five videos to go with the report that I can release in product form as well.

You can also do a webinar class or teleclasses in a live form. I like to call that the boot camp model or the mini-camp model, where you're teaching a different subject along the same lines.

Jane Button has created the Design to Market Success University. Hers began as a boot camp, a series of classes that she conducted through technology, such as webinars or teleclasses. She charges for participation. Then she records it, has it transcribed, and creates a binder with videos and/or audios. *Voilà!* A home-study course.

Generating Revenue

You charge for your time. Again I'm going back to the college professor model or the kindergarten teacher model. You're charging for your time and your experience. This is a very real model. Those are things you can create quickly.

You can create a curriculum for a teleclass. You can create a principle that you want to teach today, have a blog post or a sales letter up tomorrow, have it link to a PayPal button, and be teaching it next Monday, generating revenue for the next week. If you can get excited about generating revenue this week, raise your hand!

My husband has gotten so spoiled by information marketing that when he has a new house project or something in mind, he'll say, "What can we create in the next week or two to come up with _____ dollars?"

You can create money. It's like printing money, especially once you have your list and your audience ready to respond. It's legal. It's ethical.

It's valuable, and again, it can be immediate. This is one of the skills that I'm most excited to teach my clients.

Taking Action

Now here's the key to information marketing. Your only limitation is how much action you're willing to take. It's inexpensive, it's immediate, it's invaluable, and it's in demand.

So what's stopping you? One word—*you*. You are the only thing stopping you. You have to decide:

- What do you know?
- Whom will you market to?
- What do they want?
- What can you create quickly?

You're intelligent and you can do this.

Why not practice with some teleclasses? Why not do some audios? Why not? What is stopping you? Again, your only limitation is how much action you are willing to take.

I'm excited to see what you can get from your brain to the bank.

You may have things you've created that you just haven't put out there yet. I had to tell a client today, "Stop researching so much. Stop learning. Stop consuming and put something on the market. Hook something to your shopping cart and sell it. Put it out there."

The first dollar that you make with information marketing is absolutely the hardest and the most thrilling dollar that you make. But you have to break down the belief barrier that you have information worth charging for.

BAREFOOT ACTION STEP

Set a Deadline for *You*

**Watch the "Set a Deadline for *You*" video
at http://www.barefootexecutivevideos.com/deadlines**

I posted a question to Twitter recently, also to my mastermind Google groups, and also to a newsletter group: "If you only had thirty days to create $5,000 in your business, what strategies would you use?"

There was no shortage of strategies; people were coming up with ideas left and right. Then more than one of these people said, "Hey, wait a minute. Why am I not doing that now?"

Why are you waiting? Why aren't you working with urgency?

Don't your bills need to be paid? Mine do. Doesn't your savings need more in it? Mine does. Don't you have big events coming up or college to prepare for or medical things going on? What about an emergency account? Do you have credit card bills to pay off?

Why aren't we working with urgency? Why aren't we creating cash like we know that we can? Are you waiting for the next big launch, the next big idea, or the next Easy button? You know what? There are a couple of systems in your business that you've done once and you loved it and you celebrated and then you didn't do it again.

Teleseminars are a good example. They are great list builders, great product creators, and great cash makers. Why aren't you doing those more often? Once per quarter maybe or once a month or once every couple of weeks. Now, don't burn out, but if you know you get results from some methods, then use them, repeat them, and build your cash flow.

Why not? I don't understand why we're not working with urgency. Maybe we're not desperate enough. Maybe we're not hungry enough. Maybe we're not needy enough. Maybe we're complacent.

I challenge you today to make a plan to create $5,000 in the next thirty days in your business. I believe you can. Let me know how you do.

BAREFOOT CASE STUDY

Janet Beckers
Australia
Wonderful Web Women
www.wonderfulwebwomen.com
Business Development

"I often do collaborative projects with people who may seem to be competitors. It's just a way of finding where the win is for each person. What do you do that's different? What's unique?"

I had worked as a nurse for years and years, and I loved the contact that I had with my patients. I really liked helping people get better. I was always coming up with ideas on how we could do things better or how we could run the hospital better, how we could be doing our customer service so much better, all of these things that I wanted to implement. But when I would come with my creative ideas, which were often very practical and easy to implement, I was always coming against brick walls because there was very much this psychology of "know your place, and this is the way we do things around here." I found that very frustrating—working within a system that did not really allow people with creativity to express it.

Then I started working in nurse education; I started working at a university and I was teaching nurses. I discovered that I was actually a natural teacher and I taught through inspiring people. But again it was a big bureaucracy and very political.

Then I started working in community development. I found it something that I was actually quite good at. I liked working out what were the personal and individual motivations for different people that would motivate them to contribute their time and their energy toward a collaborative goal.

From there, I decided to start my first business. The reason why I've built my business in the way that I have is so that I can always be here for my children. We travel a lot together, thanks to my business, which gives the flexibility and the money to do that. My very first business was an art gallery online. I did the whole thing: I organized the exhibition, worked out the marketing, did the press releases, all of that sort of stuff. Anyway, it worked out really well and I loved doing it.

I ended up five years later with a lot of hard work, a lot of trying to do every course I could think of, investing—I would have invested probably about $50,000 in my education and well over $50,000 to $60,000 in making stupid mistakes and getting expensive software made and numerous Web designers. So I worked out what not to do when building an Internet business. But five years later I had made it profitable only because of a lot of sweat and an incredible amount of persistence. I ended up with artists all around Australia whom I was representing. I had their artwork on the Web site, I was selling them, making a commission on each sale, but it was a really hard way to make money. There were very few people selling original artwork on the Internet years ago. In fact whenever I did get a competitor, I would ring them up and thank them because I found the more that people got the idea that you could purchase art on the Internet, the more likely that there was not going to be a resistance to me.

My whole business now has been built on joint ventures. I often do collaborative projects with people who may seem to be competitors. It's just a way of finding where the win is for each person. What do you do that's different? What's unique?

After I had been doing it about four or five years, I thought, *I really should learn about marketing*. It hadn't really struck me that if you have a business, what you really are is a marketer. I had still been learning.

I think I found probably the hardest and most expensive way to do everything when I started out.

Well, two things I discovered. One was the concept of information products. I looked at my existing business. I had thousands of artworks, but I still had to individually sell each one, except for when I had high-end photography or prints, but usually people were wanting to buy big artworks. I thought, *Wow, I'm selling all these original things and it's great and a really impressive Web site, but I could create something small, cheap, and sell it over and over.* It was just like a bolt of lightning.

Number two was realizing that women are looking for role models: they want to find somebody they can relate to because once they can do that, then they can go, "She's like me and she's done it, so why can't I do it?" That gave me the idea for Wonderful Web Women. I have been doing that for about three and a half years now.

I'm going to be running a big event at the end of the year, and I've decided to really ramp it up. It scares the life out of me, it really does, because it's risky. I could do it a simpler way, but that's just too comfortable.

I'm just so lucky to be inspired by these amazing women who have created success and then discovering that the big thing that makes them successful has to do with their attitude. I honestly feel as if I'm hanging out with a bunch of girlfriends all the time.

Every time I push myself out of my comfort zone and do something that scares me and succeed or fail, I think, *I won't do that one again* or *I'll do this differently.* Every time I do that, the next thing—the next challenge—is not as scary. It's almost like the rungs of the ladder on the way up are getting closer together; I can step up faster.

I'm aware that I work very well under tight deadlines, so I have a little kitchen timer on my desk. I might say, "Okay, Janet, you've got to write this blog post or do this e-mail in thirty minutes," set it off, and go, go, go. It's amazing how often you can get distracted in just thirty minutes, because so many times I'll look back and think, *My time's not up, I can't do that.*

My big driving "why"? Probably my big thing, as I was saying before, what drives me is I really am devoted to helping women increase their self-confidence, their self-esteem. To me, business development and personal development are intertwined. My other big why is that I love to travel and I especially love traveling with my family and I love adventure. So, building the business the way I have with a virtual team and working from my sunroom, I'm able to travel.

Fourteen

Goods Based: Commerce or Direct Sales

You do not have to be superhuman to do what you believe in. The most important thing is for you to believe in what you are doing. Absolutely know there are people out there who want to say "yes."

—Debbi Fields, Mrs. Fields Cookies

What Can You Sell?

Another business model is e-commerce or a store. You might choose to go the physical route of selling, as in a storefront, or you could choose a form of e-commerce, where you're selling things online.

These could be products that you create and produce, software code that you write, items you buy from another supplier, or even odds and ends that you buy specifically for the purpose of reselling.

If you produce a physical something, you need to decide, "Will I sell this through a store, will I get this into manufacturing, or will I sell this online?"

Think of what you produce that you can put online. There's a little more lead time in that because you actually have to create it and put it online, a little more time involved than with a service. But you can reach a global audience online. That's another business model.

You can also check out online stores such as eBay, Etsy, or even use a drop shipper to provide goods and services shipped directly from a third-party supplier.

E-commerce can take several forms. E-commerce is goods or materials, physical things that you don't necessarily create or manufacture but that you can have drop-shipped. Some people do this through eBay or through their own sites. But it's typically related to your core experience.

You don't have to create these things. Maybe you are going to drop-ship these things on an affiliate basis. For instance, my friend Perry (Ask Mr. Video), perhaps through his site is going to link to the Flip camera or a light kit or a green screen or a teleprompter download or other things that you can get through e-commerce that are related to his niche, his expertise, and his industry.

It doesn't require much additional work for him—maybe a little setup and some quality control. Perry is not boxing these up and shipping them himself. But they are related to what he does. They are not distracting him. They are not causing him to dig an additional trench. They are simply supplementing what he already has. Does that make sense? He is using his same audience, his same reach, and creating additional streams of income.

E-commerce

Let me talk to you a little bit about e-commerce. When I talk about e-commerce, I'm not talking about Internet marketing or info products. I'm talking about a tangible something you're selling—some type of goods—not necessarily the same as with info products, where you're selling courses or coaching or audio teachings.

E-commerce can be a wide variety. Think about Amazon.com. They're the mega e-commerce solution that often comes to mind. And think about eBay, which allows people to do e-commerce in a smaller, more user-friendly way. Etsy is another one. WalMart does e-commerce in a really big way. Does it replace their stores? No, but it enhances their business and allows them to reach into some areas where they aren't physically present.

You say, "But Carrie, those are big guys. Those are big, established corporations." Well, let me talk to you about some of the little people who have integrated e-commerce into their business.

One way to integrate e-commerce is by recommending or linking to other sites. Somebody who has done that beautifully is a young friend of mine, Jason O'Neill with Pencil Bugs. Jason, a fifteen-year-old, runs Pencilbugs.com. Jason started making pencil toppers with unique personalities and adoption certificates because he felt like kids needed something fun to identify with at school or just to enjoy homework more. And he's built a site that I love. I've met Jason in person: a delightful young man whose parents are fabulous and very supportive of him.

He also is giving back. He raises funds to purchase bears for a children's hospital. What I want you to look at is the bottom of his products page. He makes all the greeting cards and the invitations; he manufactures those himself. But he's added T-shirts and tote bags and mouse pads and bibs and clocks, coffee mugs, and pockets. Now, how does he do that? Is he working with a manufacturing company? No. He markets them through Cafe Press.

You can go into Cafe Press and create an account. You upload your logo, and you pick items. You link it to your store, and you have customizable products. It's a great way to get your branding out there.

Jason and his mom are not manufacturing. Look how professional his site is. That is through cafepress.com. For instance, if I want to do T-shirts for my main event, I could upload my logo to Cafe Press, design T-shirts, and encourage attendees to grab their T-shirts before coming to the event. I could even encourage them to get creative and just sport one piece of logo merchandise, whatever they choose! They might get a bag, a cap, a mug, or a shirt. Hands-off manufacturing—you've got to love that form of e-commerce!

You can provide a small quantity of branded items for workshop attendees. You can add these as upsells to a program you are doing. I'm not sure how the commission structure works, but I know that it allows you to have a professionally manufactured product offered on your site.

The last site I want to take a look at with you is a pet store—an eco-friendly pet store called Paula's Paw Luxury that I met on Twitter. They have an e-commerce pet supply and pet treats place. They write articles and have all kinds of things you can buy. They are driven on a drop-ship basis. They probably do have a warehouse and storage.

They are primarily e-commerce business.

I don't know about you, but I am not an inventory person. I am not a person who needs all the tangibles and those details make my head spin. But what you could do is, for instance, if you are a pet blogger, you come into Paw Luxury or PetSmart or someplace like that. You sign up for their partner or affiliate program and you feature it on your site, through a button or through an advertisement. Then as you blog or add videos about what you are interested in, your traffic, or readers, will click through those buttons, which are hard-coded with a special tracking number to you, and you will earn a commission on any items they purchase. This is an excellent way to add value to your readers for things they are likely already looking for and also to add a layer of income to your online activities.

BarefootExecutive.TV is my online network that I use for my TV content. And I want to show you just a couple of things I've done. Look at the new widget that I put in for advertising. This is one way you can implement e-commerce. If I have a pet blog or am doing pet videos or green videos, I can put a square here for Paw Luxury and add an e-commerce aspect to my site through their program and I am totally hands-off.

There are many ways to add e-commerce without entirely being an e-commerce site. Another friend of ours, Kristen Arnold, was the manufacturer and designer of Tubby Bundles. She manufactured and produced towels and baby wraps for little ones. They could be customized, and they were made from a special fabric that was imported. She had lots of logistics to coordinate for the manufacturing process.

If you want to get into e-commerce where you're manufacturing, you can do that. Jane Button at design2marketsuccess.com knows more about the manufacturing aspect than I do. But these are just some examples of e-commerce. Basically, like any business model, you can start as simple and get as complicated as you want to. I'm a simple girl and prefer to keep things easy, with fewer moving parts.

Whom Can You Represent?

The direct-sales model means you are selling a product or service from a corporate entity but you are an independent contractor. There are many direct-sales companies, including Longaberger Baskets, BeautiControl, Tupperware, and DK Books. There are Discovery Toys, Avon, Mary Kay, Gold Canyon Candles, PartyLite, Premier Jewelry, and on and on and on.

There are even some nontangible product options, such as Legal Aid, Travel, and Send Out Cards. Look for a product or service that appeals to you and that you either use already or can get excited about. Do your research on reported complaints and reputation in the industry. Then sign up, go through your training, and focus on massive action and results!

Direct sales is a very viable business model and one that works for thousands and thousands of people. The attraction to direct sales for many work-at-home starters is the low startup cost, the ability to function without a storefront, and a turnkey business model. In many cases, you even have a recommended supplier for business cards, a company-provided Web site, and free or low-cost training through the corporate approved trainers.

Perhaps even more important than the above benefits, there is a proven product; you do not have to create something or come up with an original idea. The market has already been proven; someone else has the risk and the burden of production.

I have several great friends who are making mid to high six figures in direct sales. Again, like every business model, this is a great option, but one you need to spend some time and focus on in order to see real results.

BAREFOOT ACTION STEP

You Cannot Do It All Alone!

The best executive is the one who has sense enough to pick good men to do what he wants done, and self-restraint enough to keep from meddling with them while they do it.

—**Theodore Roosevelt**

**Watch the "You Cannot Do It All Alone!" video
at http://www.barefootexecutivevideos.com/delegate**

I want to talk to you a little bit about delegation, multiplying your efforts so you can exponentially increase your income. Now, before you tune me out, before you say, "Oh, I've heard all that before," let me tell you some comments I get on my site.

People say, "Carrie, I could do what you do, I could make what you make, I could juggle what you juggle if I had your husband. If my husband was supportive like your husband, if he did the books like your husband, or helped with the kids, I could do that."

"If I had a housekeeper I could do that. If I had somebody doing my transcription I could do that. If I had somebody helping with my Web design I could do that." They say, "If I had what you had, I could do that."

I didn't start with the team that I have. I started with me. And yes, I have a husband who is helpful and supportive. What I saw very quickly is that I can only do so much. I can do it all and I can do a pretty good job on most of it, but I can only do so much directly related to the income-producing activities of my business.

At one point I asked, "Is it worth it for me to fold the towels or put away the clothes or do all the house cleaning, or would it be better for me to pay someone?" I don't know what the market bears in your area, but say I'm paying ten dollars an hour for a housekeeper or somebody to help with the laundry, and I know that if I'm focusing on bringing in new clients, perhaps I could be making fifty, one hundred, or two hundred dollars an hour.

Maybe she doesn't do the laundry like we would do it, maybe the housekeeper doesn't do things exactly the way I would; it's okay—it's getting done and I'm able to focus on my business.

Maybe, just maybe, I want to spend that time with Baby Barefoot and the kids. Maybe it's family time and we want to go to the park or spend some time together. What's that worth? Is it worth thirty dollars for the three hours I'm paying her to clean the house instead of us spending all day on it? Absolutely. It's worth it.

If you are being blocked because you don't have enough time, you need to find a way to funnel some of that income toward some help. Now, be smart about your help. Be savvy about what you're outsourcing and how you're doing it. If you are constantly drained, constantly tired, can't get it all done, and you're beginning to resent it, then you need to outsource some things.

Another reason I need to outsource is because I need to be focused on the things I love, the things that are most profitable, and the things that I can do more quickly. Dan Sullivan, founder of Strategic Coach, says for maximum profitability and growth, I need to be focusing within my "Unique Ability."

I can work on a Web page for two hours and do a good job, but maybe my tech support team can do the same thing in fifteen to thirty minutes because they're not distracted by other things, they're not emotionally attached to it, and they're not worrying about getting it absolutely beautiful, perfect, and wonderful; they're getting it working.

Is it worth spending money for a tech team to make sure they have all the motors running behind the face of the business while I get to be the face of the business, creating the things that turn the wheels? You need to look at those things.

"Carrie, I can't afford to do those things in my business right now." I say you can't afford not to. Find one thing to delegate this week. Get out a piece of paper. One trick I always teach is to put all the things on half of the page that nobody can do but you, meaning coaching calls, product orders, or product consultations, whatever your business is, whatever you have to do that cannot be delivered by somebody else. Write those things on the left-hand side of the paper.

Anything someone else can do, put on the right-hand side. Yes, household things as well as business things. Laundry, housekeeping, cooking, shopping, dropping off product orders, taking things to the post office, mailing packages, copying newsletters, whatever it might be, put that on the right-hand side. Then group the things someone else can do according to categories—personal, household, financial, or technical. Find or make a way to create some outsourcing for as many of those things as possible.

There are so many affordable outsourcing solutions right now. There is somebody who is willing to clean your house for a really nominal fee. Somebody is willing to do your technical work for you affordably. If you can't find somebody in the technical area, ask me who I recommend. Somebody is willing to help you make deliveries and do post office stuff. Maybe there is a senior in your community or a stay-at-home mom who is willing to do those things for much less per hour than what you are being paid.

I challenge you to take some of the load off. I am working fewer days right now than I have in a long time. I do have several businesses, so I stay pretty busy, but I'm cutting back on my time. I'm ramping up my outsourcing in some really smart ways—and it's freeing my creative spirit, my energy, my love for my business again so that I'm not bogged down.

So, don't say to me, "If I just had the CFO that you have I could do what you do." Take a step in the right direction and start outsourcing the things that don't immediately require your personal attention.

BAREFOOT CASE STUDY

David Frey
Texas
Send Out Cards
MarketingBestPractices.com
Online Marketing

"If it was to be, it was up to me."

At twenty-seven years of age, after spending six years in the U.S. Navy and two years as a missionary in Bolivia, I decided to go to college. After all, everyone told me that to get a good-paying job, I had to have a college degree. I decided to study accounting because it was a good, solid business degree.

At the age of thirty-seven, I received my master's degree in accounting. While in college, everyone wanted to go to work for the big consulting firms. The hiring process was very competitive. For a college superstar, working at a big-name consulting firm was the ultimate achievement. It represented achievement, success, and brilliance. Every one of my college friends desperately wanted to get hired by one of the big consulting firms, but unfortunately, few were accepted. When it came time for the interview process, I interviewed with all five of the biggest consulting firms. When the dust had settled, all five offered me a job. I was ecstatic!

When I entered the world of consulting I envisioned power meetings, jet-setting consulting gigs, C-level introductions, and, of course, making a lot of money. The reality was that I sometimes worked eighty-hour weeks, often worked five days a week out of town, and did a lot of menial tasks. As I moved up the corporate ladder, my job assignments became more meaningful, but the work hours never slowed down. The big consulting firms expected you to be married to them. Your life was theirs.

Oftentimes I only saw my wife and small children on the weekends. When I was in town, I got up at 5:30 a.m. and drove for an hour into the city and didn't get home till 7:00 or later at night, just in time to say good night to my kids. The firm rarely allowed me to take the time off I wanted, and I don't recall ever being able to attend a parent-teacher meeting or a school activity with my kids.

Eventually I took a job with a corporation as a senior vice president of a five-hundred-million-dollar company. I made a lot more money but rarely had the time to spend it with my family. I eventually came to the conclusion, "What good was having a high-flying, high-paying job when it robbed you of any sort of personal life?"

And then the day came—the day that changed my life forever. I got fired. My company merged with another company and my position was given to the person in the takeover company.

I went online to research my next job. Immediately I was enthralled with what I saw. I came across people selling e-books and courses. I told myself: *I can do this!* And that was the beginning of www.MarketingBestPractices .com. I started a little e-mail newsletter called The Small Business Marketing Best Practices newsletter. It went out every week and gave tips and strategies about how to market a small business. Fast-forward to today: more than seventy thousand small business owners around the world receive my newsletter in more than forty different countries. I also run several other Internet-based properties in different markets.

But it wasn't easy. I had to retool my skills, readjust my brain to the entrepreneurial realization that "if it was to be, it was up to me." It took me more than a year of learning how to do online marketing before I ever made a penny from my new business. Many times it was very frustrating, but I never thought of quitting and going back to the grind of the corporate world. To me, that was insanity. Every minute of frustration and sacrifice I experienced to achieve financial freedom was worth it.

Today I have a small office about five minutes from my home that I go in to a couple of days a week. I have a few employees who help me in the business and several outsourcers who help me do different tasks. I spend about two to three months a year traveling around the world. I attend every one of my kids' activities, whether it's during the day, evening, or on the weekend.

I donate my time to the local Boy Scouts and am involved in building schools in third world countries. I never wake up to an alarm clock in the morning and just finished running a marathon with my wife in Athens, Greece. I have freedom to do what I want, where I want, how I want, and with whom I want. Whether I'm working or playing, my income never stops. Now, who wouldn't want that type of life?

Looking back, I thank God I got fired! It was the best thing that's ever happened to me.

Fifteen

Referral Based:
Commission or Affiliate Marketing

I chose to be an active participant in my life rather than
a spectator.

—Robin McGraw

et's talk about a stream that we might call passive income or automated income. You may not be familiar with this model, so let me introduce you to affiliate income or commission-based income.

This is a stream of income that I leverage to more than six figures a year currently, and, yes, I know several individuals who use affiliate income as their primary source of revenue. I choose to use it as a supplement. Because of the leverage I have with my current audience, my current customers, I can recommend other products and services that I get a thank-you check for.

For example, maybe I find a really great tech-assist service and I'm using them for all my Web-based needs, and I recommend them to my audience. Subsequently, if I'm on their affiliate or partner program, I get a thank-you check based on other people using them too. You may call it a referral gift or a sales incentive.

Monthly as I'm focusing on different topics of interest in business or self-development, I recommend products or services that I don't provide, but that are related to the ongoing discussions and education. If my listeners, readers, or viewers choose to purchase, then I earn an income supplement. I disclose that fact per FTC guidelines and there is no hidden agenda. I make it a policy only to recommend things or folks that I personally use or know and that have a great guarantee policy.

My affiliate commissions are now in the $8,000–$10,000 range monthly because of steady implementation and because my audience trusts me. I don't recommend anything based on the commission, but because I believe in it. The commission is just a thank you, not my primary motive.

Some popular affiliate programs you might have heard of:

- Amazon.com
- Zappos.com
- PayPal.com

Some affiliate marketplaces where you can find other products by a wide variety of merchants:

- ClickBank.com
- Commission Junction

For a very practical example, perhaps you have a parenting blog and you have several books you like to recommend. Sign up for Amazon's partner program and put the special coded affiliate link or widget or image on your blog. When your readers see that recommendation, if they click and buy at some point, it goes into an Amazon commission account for you. It really can be that simple.

Affiliate marketing is simply earning a commission on something that you recommend. So when you click on an Amazon book that's on somebody's blog, the blogger is earning a commission on that. Is that sleazy? Is that icky? No, they're recommending it to you. The reason you saw it, the reason you knew you were going to like it or got curious about it was that a person used his or her virtual real estate to recommend the book and that is perfectly legitimate. My advice is that if you feel the need to add a product or a service as a stream of income, go straight to affiliate marketing. It can be very lucrative and it's one of my favorite strengths.

Conversely, when you have something to offer to the marketplace, you can create an affiliate program and have other influencers promote you, but right now, we want to focus on you adding this as a stream of simple income.

The huge difference between doing this offline or online is that offline you tend to make 5, 10, and maybe as high as 20 percent with a physical product. But when you're talking about digital products and downloadables, the average product online digitally allows you to get a 50 percent commission. And most serious affiliate promotions give you a 75 percent commission. And so here you are, able to earn this huge commission off a product that you sell. To be able to do that offline, you're going to have to sell so many more units than you are online.

In order to get folks to *see* your recommendations and offers, however, you're going to have to do some marketing—as in promotion. If you've got a site or you've got a blog or if you are active in social media, then you are ahead of the game.

You can use your current space to do promotions, and it's so easy and quick to be able to get out there and find some simple commission-based projects that are going to align with what you're already doing. Often with affiliate marketing, people want to get out there and find something new and fresh. Reaching so far outside of what they're already doing doesn't make sense. (Remember the mistakes in developing income streams? Chasing the hot, trendy, and unrelated also applies here.)

Start from the space that you're already known for and you're already working in, and choose some affiliate products that are going to allow you to do that. This concept is pretty exciting to me because there are so many advantages.

Curiosity Marketing

You want people to be thinking, *What happens next?* For instance, I want your customers or recruits or team to wonder what you're up to. What is that Renée going to do now? What's up with her? There needs to be some suspense built in. I think this is very important. You need to have *fun*. Do I need to repeat it, or did you get that? You need to have *fun*.

People want to do business with someone they can have fun with, regardless of your business model. You have to start and keep it going. You can't question yourself, your validity, your market, your worth, will this work, et cetera. Only you can make this happen.

And once you get this great funnel in place of online list building, social media, live events, and then following up with people over and over and building relationships, you will be unstoppable, absolutely unstoppable. I don't care if your business is online or offline, established or new, you will be unstoppable.

BAREFOOT ACTION STEP

Relationships

People don't care how much you know until they know how much you care.
—Theodore Roosevelt

**Watch the "Relationships" video
at http://www.barefootexecutivevideos.com/relationships**

Relationships are always relevant, and that's true now in business more than ever. I want to talk to you about your relationship with your audience, your list, your customers, and also your relationship in the marketplace with your associates, your joint venture partners, the other marketers in your field, and even like-minded business owners who are not necessarily in your market.

I totally believe that you could take away my list, you could take away all the products I've created, and I could rebuild a business in six to seven weeks based on relationships that I have in the field.

I believe that I could build up a list again very quickly through social media and through the relationships that I have with other people. I believe that I could promote their products, I believe that I could cocreate products, or I could speak on stages until I got back on my feet because of the relationships that I have built.

If you know me, if you've met me personally, you know I'm serious about relationship building. I love the people who are close to me, and I surround myself closely with people who have high integrity, high values, high drive, achievement, and goals.

So I want you to work on building relationships whether you're in a coaching group, a mastermind group, or whether you're just on forums and social media where you gather a group around you. Your mom always said, "Birds of a feather flock together." That's true, and I want you to be stretching out.

Build those relationships. Don't just name-drop and say, "I know so-and-so," but build the relationship. It might take the effort of sending a card, a postcard, a gift, placing a phone call just to leave a message, "I was thinking about you," posting something on a Facebook wall, or sending an e-mail just because.

I got an e-mail this morning from someone in one of my close circles who asked, "Carrie, how can I help you? What is something I can help you with?" The sad truth of the matter is I don't get that offer very much. I get a lot of e-mails and calls from people who want to know how I can help them, what I can do for them, how I can promote them to my list, or help them get their foot in the door.

I rarely, and I mean like three times in the past six months, have someone who says, "What can I do for you? Please let me know what I can do for you." I'm not telling you this so you will send me an e-mail or a post; I'm saying that's how you build solid relationships and that's how you can set yourself apart from the norm. And when you build relationships with other people, then they're going to ask, "How can I help you?"

Regarding your customers and your list, I just want to tell you a quick story about my relationship with my list. My list trusts me, my audience trusts me, and therefore when I promote something I feel strongly about, they tend to respond if it's a good fit for them. I don't sugarcoat things, I don't hype things, but I had a promotion recently where I promoted a good friend and a product that I strongly believed in and I'm using for myself.

After the launch I did for this person, he launched it through several guru lists, big lists, and hypersellers. I'm going to toot my horn, and the truth is I'm going to toot the horn of the relationship I have with my list. My list was responsible for more than half of the volume that he did during that period—more than half.

My list has not been built solely on Internet marketing, so I only mailed part of my list about it, only the really solid Internet business builders that might be interested. Am I proud of that? I'm very proud of that because what that says to me is that my list trusts me, they trust the people I trust, and they take our relationship seriously and know I do too.

How can you build a great relationship with your list? Be careful who you promote, what you promote, how often you promote, and make sure you give your list good stuff—good content, good resources, good stories, good illustrations and examples. Be applicable, relevant, resourceful, and respected.

BAREFOOT CASE STUDY

Nicole Dean
Florida
NicoleOnTheNet.com
Stay-at-Home Mom and Full-Time Affiliate Marketer

"Keep in mind both your financial goals and your lifestyle goals so you can build a future that is exactly what you're dreaming of now."

My story starts with having lots of interesting jobs before I found my true passion—online business. I'm married with two children, a thirteen-year-old and a nine-year-old. Besides our own two puppies, we foster golden retrievers through a rescue—so there's always an extra fuzzy friend around.

My husband was laid off just three weeks after our younger child was born. It was a serious wake-up call when I saw how stressful that was on him—and the fact that all of the financial responsibility had been on his shoulders. (I was a stay-at-home mom at the time.) Our income went from a very nice income to zero overnight.

I vowed that day that we'd take control over our financial situation and never have our future be in the hands of a corporation. Thankfully, with hard work (and some tears), I was able to make that dream a reality. Now I earn more money than I ever could at a day job. My husband and mother joined me in the business and are able to spend time doing what they love because of the flexibility of the business.

My main "why" is one simple quote that I heard a long time ago and have no idea who to attribute it to. "The days are long, but the years are short."

I've learned the value of taking chances and the money that comes when you step outside of your comfort zone. And I wish I'd understood that I needed to keep in mind not only the money I wanted but also the lifestyle I wanted at the same time. Now I filter the information I receive and only learn from positive, warm people who are living the lifestyle that I want. I don't want a gazillion dollars if it means that I can't go to the beach with my kids. I don't want to be trapped at my computer—or to have to have my phone with me at all times. So, as you're building your business, keep in mind both your financial goals and your lifestyle goals so you can build a future that is exactly what you're dreaming of now.

Sixteen

Multiple Streams of Income

That some achieve great success is proof to all that others can achieve it as well.

—Abraham Lincoln

I had three children and one on the way and was CEO of a high six-figure business from home and a husband working at home full-time with me. Things were great. While traveling, however, my friend Ann Vertel and I decided to attend a conference about the benefits of multiple streams of income. This was a bit of a foreign concept to me, and after all, why fragment myself when the company was doing so well?

My company was focused on a very specific niched-down boutique industry that, while profitable, was a little risky since my income was based solely on serving this one market. If something happened in that market (like a recession or corporate takeover), then my income could vanish literally overnight.

While I was at this conference, I was not starry-eyed at the sales pitches of the real estate investors, the instant-solution finders, or the investment opportunities, but a very powerful thought was planted in my mind that I needed to divert a stream of income and not have all my eggs in one basket, so to speak. Rather than jump around from income op to income op, I decided to take my own advice mentioned in earlier chapters and build on what I already knew instead of radically changing directions.

As a result of adding information products and coaching to my streams of income in the service business, when the economic downturn slashed my existing business by *half*, my overall income was unaffected because of the cushion I'd put into place.

Again, I will caution you not to divert into multiple streams before you have something radically and ridiculously profitable. To fragment yourself before you're at comfortable profit is self-defeating. Wait until you have the systems and security in place before you try to duplicate this in other areas.

Okay, so who does this apply to?

- Maybe you are already profitable in business.
- Maybe you are a professional with a lucrative practice, but you are working too many hours.
- Maybe you are frustrated with your current career track and you want to begin an income stream on the side to cushion your transition.
- Maybe you are looking for additional income to achieve a certain goal, such as your kids' college, a vacation, an investment, a wedding, or retirement planning.

Either way, all of the prior rules apply. You investigate what your skill sets are and what your knowledge, your time, space, and software are. And you evaluate how you can leverage one of the five models I just discussed in addition to what you are currently doing.

Adding a stream of income doesn't have to require a big investment of time or money. This doesn't even necessarily require a huge learning curve. You can apply the methodical process of asking yourself the assessment questions of whom will you serve, what do you know, and how will you deliver it—then do it.

Oversimplified? I don't think so. Just think of how you can serve from one to many in this new way and how you will charge for it.

BAREFOOT ACTION STEP

Prepare, Plan, Produce

It is better to be prepared for an opportunity and not have one than to have an opportunity and not be prepared.

—Whitney M. Young Jr.

**Watch the "Prepare, Plan, Produce" video
at http://www.barefootexecutivevideos.com/productive**

One thing I've noticed while shooting videos today is that you must prepare yourself for the best possible success. My camera batteries died in the middle of a video, and I had to leave to find batteries, which weren't where I thought they were. So I wasted a lot of time when shooting the videos should have been a fast and easy thing for me to do.

Sometimes I say, "Oh, I'll jump up while this file is downloading and fix myself another cup of coffee." I get up and notice that the creamer is empty, but the container is still sitting there. So I throw away the container and get a new one and open it.

Then I notice that the sweetener needs to be refilled, so I restock that. Then I notice there are dirty dishes on the counter, so I handle that. By the time I get back to my work after that quick cup of coffee, it's taken me thirty to forty-five minutes of being distracted because I didn't set myself up for the most efficient use of my time, the most effective use of my time, or the best systems.

How does this apply to your work? One, as I should have with my camera batteries, make sure your electronics are backed up, charged up, and ready to go. Make sure you have the right supplies close to your workstation. Make sure your workplace is neat and orderly in a way that you can function efficiently.

I've spent the last few days putting some bookshelves in, getting some things organized, and even purging some things. Maybe you also need to give yourself permission to let go of stuff and clutter. I'm setting myself up with some space, a lack of chaos, and things in easy reach and organized best for me.

That helps me, it calms me internally, and it helps me not feel so flustered all the time. The same is true of your computer. Do you have things in folders that make sense to you filed away? Do you have things backed up on your computer? I know it has set me back before when I thought I was backed up and I wasn't.

How are you setting yourself up with the most effective systems possible, the best organization? I am not organized by nature, but in my workspace and during my work time I try to pay close attention to organization. I just upgraded my desk to have more surface area. My other desk only had room for my computer, so I didn't have room for a calendar or supplies, and I was constantly juggling and constantly stacking. It wasn't a good situation.

Today give yourself permission to take about thirty minutes and evaluate what's working, what's not working, and how you can set things up differently. You don't have to make the changes today, but make a list of what would help you be more efficient and effective in the future.

BAREFOOT CASE STUDY

Bryan C. Binkholder
St. Louis, Missouri
www.TheFinancialCoach.com
The Financial Coach Financial Services

"You can do it and you can understand it!"

As a schoolteacher in the early 1990s, I quickly found out that the system wasn't for me. It was at this point that my life turned and I embraced my faith and a new purpose. That purpose was to help others in business. Not knowing what that exactly was, I ventured into many areas, including vending machines and sales. My passion, however, was finances and money.

I first became a financial advisor part-time. Then, I started an educational consulting company and through its sales my wife and I got completely out of debt (house, cars, credit cards, everything). At the same time I created an insurance agency with telemarketers and we ran an agency of reps. That agency morphed into seminar marketing and financial advising for retirees because my parents had experienced catastrophic loss in their financial life. Because of faulty advice, they had lost more than $100,000 of assets, which was no small amount to them.

From here, my entire focus became one designed to educate and instruct people in finances and planning. Today the Financial Coach has products and services for individuals of all backgrounds and needs. From debt elimination to learning how investing really works and the steps to successfully implement a retirement plan, the Financial Coach addresses it all. Coupled with our radio show, the *Financial Coach Show*, the message to people is clear: you can do it and you can understand it! I have a passion to help others and I know a gift God has given me is educating people in a practical manner.

PART FOUR RECAP

There is no cookie-cutter business system that works for everyone, and there is no "set" model that I suggest for instant success. Rather, I believe you should look at the models I've mentioned and see which is a best fit for you to focus on. You might choose to pursue multiple models later on, but you need to get your first one to extreme profit before you start distracting yourself.

Service Based: Whom can you serve and how? This is one of the fastest and lowest-cost options. I believe almost anyone can be generating cash quickly with a service-based business. My mom was a great example of this my entire life, using her skills as a pianist, a seamstress, and now as a typist to generate extra funds for our family.

Expertise Based: What have you done, and what do you know that is specialized? Is there a population that you can serve as a coach or consultant? Coaches are not the same as consultants and vice versa, but these are both powerful models that capitalize on your experience and your skill set.

Knowledge Based: Take your brain to the bank! If you can write or talk, you can create information products based on your past and present. Books, audios, videos, courses, and even live events fall into the information category. And whether you realize it or not, you are a treasure trove that someone else is looking for. Your experience is valuable. Let's get it out there.

Goods Based: Should you create something? Do you want to represent a product that already exists? Selling a tangible good is commerce, and there is a huge range of opportunity from eBay to self-driven sites for those of you who are interested in creating goods, representing a big company and their product line, or even seeking and finding goods like antiques, collectibles, and more.

Referral Based: Also called affiliate marketing, this is being paid for recommending products and services that someone else provides to your audience. A viable model along with another or as a stand-alone, this adds about six figures to my income a year, and you can do this with zero inventory, no fulfillment, no customer service, and still earn a nice income.

Multiple Streams of Income: I hesitate to draw attention to this one for fear that it will distract you, but if you already have a great stream of income, this might be something to consider—adding one of the models above to what you already have in the works for layering of your income.

Part Five

The Marketplace

Seventeen

Who Wants What You Have?

The woman who can create her own job is the woman who will win fame and fortune.

—Amelia Earhart

This chapter is what's going to keep your mind spinning this afternoon and tonight. I will apologize in advance for giving you "idea insomnia."

- What ideas are inside of you?
- What ideas are you passionate about?
- What ideas keep you up at night?

What are you interested in? Is it boating or fine wines or travel or romance novels or parenting or homeschooling or fashion? What is it that really excites you? Is it golf, software, bass fishing, or all things related to adoption?

I'm really passionate about adoption. If I had my way, I would adopt again right now. I have clients in the adoption process, I have clients who are adoption coaches, and I am always open to helping parentless children. My husband says I have to channel my passion into funding, that we have a full house, and my next adoption will have to be with my "next" husband. (Humph.)

Maybe you're into relaxing and romantic vacations and you want to blog about that and recommend hideaways to people. Maybe you're really passionate about big families and you want to talk about budget-saving things for big families or interests for big families. Anything that you have inside of you can be turned into a niche.

Now let's talk about the ideas that are outside of you. Look around. Go to the grocery store and look at the magazine aisle. Who has a magazine specifically for them? If they have a magazine, then they can support a market or niche.

Here's something that Yanik Silver, author of *Moonlighting on the Internet*, taught me: Right before you go to bed, ask yourself a question: What is a market I would love to serve? What is a market that I could be really passionate about?

Ask yourself a big question right before you go to bed. You may be surprised at how your mind goes into action to answer that question. It will sometimes wake you up, and when you wake up, write it down. Write it down and go back to sleep. Jack Canfield and Mark Victor Hansen credit this method with their famous Chicken Soup for the Soul series.

Your mind doesn't like unanswered questions, so give it the blanks to fill in and let it get busy. Then in the morning you may wake up and think: *Oh, my goodness. That was the stupidest idea ever.* That's okay, but what if it was a really good idea and you didn't write it down? What ideas are inside of you and what ideas are outside of you? That's one way to start finding your niche.

My mentor and friend Zig Ziglar has taught me to keep a notepad by the bedside so that no matter what time of night it is, I can write down that great idea and revisit it in the morning. He has been doing that himself for well over fifty years, and I'd say it has served him well. Wouldn't you agree?

Before you act on those ideas, do not start writing your novel based on bass fishing vacations until you've done some market research. Consider your market because your market has money. Think of your market, the one you're the most passionate about right now—whether it's scrapbooking or virtual assistants or Christian home schools or real estate; or hunting, knitting, or videography, think right now:

- *Does your market have money?* Do they have income to spend? For example, hobby markets tend to spend no matter the economy. Markets with high affinity or love for their leader (think of rock stars, actors, huge household-name figures), followers of these will spend also.

- *Are they reachable online or off?* Can you get to your market and can they find you? If you're getting red flags about your market already, you need to reevaluate. You'd only be banging your head up against the wall. You may have the perfect product for your market, but if they can't find you, they aren't reachable through low-cost online, direct mail, or social media methods. And if they don't have discretionary income, then I say, let's save them for later. Let's go for low-hanging fruit first and develop a primary income stream and system for you that you can replicate on that particular market later when you have the luxury of spending time and money finding them and getting them to respond.

- *Is there pain you can solve for someone?* Everyone has pain. Do you have a solution for them? Don't just think about physical pain, but emotional, spiritual, weight, health, and time. What are you solving for them?

Market pain: My skinny jeans don't fit anymore; I have this spare tire (or muffin top).

Solution: Craig Ballantyne's Turbulence Training: fitness without boring cardio, fast results, simple solutions.

Market pain: We're in debt and stressed-out from bill collectors calling.

Solution: Dave Ramsey, Financial Peace University.

Market pain: My golf swing stinks and is even causing physical trauma.

Solution: Justin Tupper introduced Peak Performance Golf Swing.

Market pain: My house is a mess and I'm overwhelmed.

Solution: The Fly Lady has a system and online guidance to free you from your chaos.

Market pain: I have fast-food guilt but don't know where to start for meal times.

Solution: Leanne Ely with SavingDinner.com provides meal plans and shopping lists.

Market pain: I want to fix some things around the house or hire a contractor.

Solution: Tim Carter founded AsktheBuilder.com to help.

Market pain: I feel as if I'm always struggling to get new clients or keep appointments.

Solution: Michael Port teaches "Book Yourself Solid" and provides a supportive software.

Market pain: I need more blog ideas and topics to write about. I have writer's block.

Solution: Chris Brogan developed Blog Topics, a weekly idea generator for bloggers.

How can you frame your market into a series of primary pain and solutions?

People will spend more money—listen, this is gold—they will spend more money to solve their problem and to fix pain than they will for prevention, pleasure, or privilege. That's just the way they tie their wallet to it.

Don't give your market too much credit. Weight loss will always outsell wellness. Debt freedom will also outsell smart investing or saving strategies. Often we want them to pay to stay smart when, really, they are more anxious and willing to pay to fix stupid. That seems harsh, but let's talk about some markets that have some heavy pain involved.

weight loss	divorce recovery
behavior problems with children	special-needs kids
finding a date or mate	infertility
adoption	debt recovery
credit repair	job seeking
chronic pain	low sex drive
marital distress	terminal illness
job loss	income loss

But maybe there's no pain. Maybe there's no problem. Then let's talk about your rabid, your passionate, your fanatical markets. Those are people like golfers, scrapbookers, bass fishermen, boaters, gamers, and photographers—people who are into trinkets and toys and things they're excited about.

I know men who will begrudge their wives going to the store without coupons but yet they won't think anything about dropping $150 at the golf course every Saturday because "it's how I unwind from my week."

I have to admit that I'm pretty frugal. (Not as frugal as my husband, but again, that is a topic for a different book.) But having managed my finances into extreme debt, one does learn a few things along the way, and the most powerful lesson was "I will never be in that spot again due to mismanagement!"

I'm not a brand shopper for clothes, shoes, or household furnishings. I know what I like, but I'm not excessive or brand conscious. When it comes to travel or experiential things for my family, friends, and me, however, I don't think twice about spending. So I might buy a pair of dress boots marked down to $37 at Kohl's, but I didn't skimp on game tickets when our beloved Texas Rangers brought the World Series to Texas in 2010! (I even sent my parents and my father-in-law, and my husband got to take his best friend and go twice.)

I prefer to take my family to a matinee movie when it's possible, but I'm also taking my oldest daughter on a tour of Venice, Vienna, and Paris on a school trip during summer break. I said yes and planned on going along before I even had final pricing. Those experiential things are what I'm passionate about, and *passion* is what you need to find out about your market, if it isn't a pain-driven market.

Whatever is closest to us and whatever we're passionate about, that's where we spend our money. Parents will skimp on themselves but spend lavishly on their kids. We will deprive ourselves but gift generously to our siblings and parents. You probably know folks who drive an old car but pull a really great boat with it. Or folks whose home is in need of expansion or updating, but they have a vacation home too. What about the family who says they are struggling with money but have every high-tech phone, gaming system, and hundreds of channels on their streaming television?

We spend on what is important to us. Find out what your audience thinks is important and how you can fill those needs.

We have family friends who have five children and I don't know how they live on their income. He is a hospital chaplain and she stays home with the kids, teaching part-time preschool two days a week. They vacation every year as a family, and they've internationally adopted twice and paid cash because by living frugally they save money for something that they're passionate and excited about. What you have to do, if you're not in a market that's solving problems or solving pain for somebody, is find a rabid, fanatical group. (I mean rabid and fanatical in the nicest possible way.)

Jane Button is a client of mine who is teaching people how to turn their crafts and their handy skills into businesses. She and her Glue Gun Lady are taking an army of quilters, knitters, crocheters, sewers, those people who create and are good with that stuff, and turning them into crafters for cash. My mom is a great example of this. I tell you what—she has more fabric in her house than she can ever sew in two lifetimes. My dad calls it house insulation, but she's a fabric collector for those potential ideas and potential projects—just in case she needs them. She calls it her "stash."

Every seamstress reading this will be nodding as she reads. She understands. A seamstress will spend money on patterns and fabric while cutting out coupons for peanut butter and buying the whole chicken because the boneless breasts are too expensive. On travels, the seamstress always knows where to find the fabric stores, no matter what city, state, or country. That's a market.

Let's talk about tangible items to help you further with this connection. Because I'm unaffected by this habit, I love to poke fun at the fanaticism for shoes and handbags. Look at the people spending money on name-brand shoes and bags in a down market—it's just what those people are passionate about. As a side note, I used to think this was a "girl" habit—but I've since met many men who have dozens and dozens of designer shoes and laptop bags, iPad covers, and carry-ons, so I have to cut the girls some slack here.

- Does your market have money? That's nonnegotiable.
- Will they spend it? Also, nonnegotiable.
- Are they reachable? Nonnegotiable.

Then the last two are kind of interchangeable:

- Is there a need or pain?
- Is your market passionate or fanatical?

Look internally for ideas, look externally for ideas, consider your market, and do your research. Then you take action. You don't go back and research some more. You don't overthink it. You don't get stressed about it. I never get over being scared or afraid—I just take action in spite of it. You can be "scared and broke" or "afraid and well paid." I prefer to be paid, thank you very much. Take action!

But . . . But . . . But I'm Not an Expert

Who am I? I'm not an expert. My friend Valerie Young has written a book called *The Imposter Syndrome*. This is fear based and also a reason many people give themselves as an excuse for not acting. "Carrie, why should they listen to me? Why should they want to hear what I have to say? Why should they read my e-mails?"

I will tell you what was said about Mount Everest: because it's there.

The fact that you take the time to build a list and take the time to publish a newsletter, the fact that you take the time to name your brand or build a Web site sets you apart. It makes you published. It makes you an authority. It makes you an action taker.

My four-year-old doesn't let the seven-year-old teach her how to tie her shoes because she has a certificate in it or has been published about it or has been featured on television about it or has won an award. Lily asks Catie to help her out because Catie's shoes are tied, she's been tying them for a while, and she's someone Lily trusts—and because she is close by, accessible.

So you have to take action, get a blog, and set yourself apart and be published. It used to be harder because you had to have a book or you had to be published in a magazine. You know what? I wasn't about to wait for somebody else to publish me. Before I had this book contract, I published myself, blogged, and shot videos. I e-mailed my audience and made myself an authority. The fact of the matter is, you are more experienced than the majority of listeners sitting across the table from you.

Here's the big secret. If they know more than you and are more experienced than you, then they are probably not going to stay on your list or not going to ask you for help. For instance, dance teachers of beginners would never hold a class if they were worried that there were more-advanced dancers in the world. They realize there are advanced dancers. But they are serving the market of beginning dancers. The advanced dancers will go elsewhere, as they should.

You will filter out those people. People coming to you are the people looking for answers, not the people looking to spread their own knowledge. You are an expert. Embrace that.

You are the authority. You are credible. You are going to show them you are credible with the articles that you write from the research you continue to do and the experts you align yourself with. You are the expert.

- What do people constantly ask you about?
- What do you find yourself readily giving advice about—even without being asked sometimes?
- What questions are you answering in your e-mail box or on your Facebook page?
- What periodicals do you read?
- What books do you buy first?

My dad is a pretty quiet guy, but if the conversation comes around to search and rescue or aircraft or Coast Guard or anything coastal, my dad is the chattiest guy in the room. The same if it comes to evangelism or mission work—he will jump up and start contributing to the conversation.

My husband can talk about bass fishing or golf or numbers and accounting and some of the financial aspects of our businesses that I have no idea about.

My mom can do the same with all things related to fabric, needles, and threads.

I have a brother who knows scads about construction and design, one who follows the investing markets and financial trends closely, and another who is a sports nut.

We all have an expertise.

My son is extremely knowledgeable about marine life in all forms, my eldest daughter is a sketch artist and instrumental musician, my seven-year-old knows show tunes and musicals like the back of her hand, and I think you can see—we all have an expertise, no matter our age, our income, or our "credentials."

I'm always engaged in some type of conversation (according to those who love and tease me), but there are things that I enthusiastically jump in for—usually about weight loss or getting out of debt or adoption or working at home or special-needs kids, our experience homeschooling or juggling four kids or time management or delegation or working-smart systems. I'm a recovered scrapbooker and cross-stitcher. I'm kind of a geek about technology and software, and I'm a travelaholic. Those are all things in which I have an interest and could spend some time developing my expertise. Expertise is based on experience with a subject—not a degree, a certificate, or anyone waving a magic wand over you and declaring you qualified.

There are things that you know about because of your life experience. What do you find yourself thinking about most often? What setbacks have you overcome?

I was sharing with someone today who has a premature baby with some medical challenges. I was able to share my mom's story. I told my mom about the baby, too, and she said, "Wow. That takes me back about thirty-six years." That's because the story was very similar to when I was born several weeks early and in ICU. So, what life experiences have you had that set you apart?

People want to know. People cannot believe that I have lost one hundred pounds. They can't believe that I haven't monetized that yet and haven't turned that into an info product. You know, the adoption—I haven't monetized that. I do weave it into my story, but that's not a niche I have pursued a lot yet.

A client of mine, Patty, was a special education teacher. Since I'm the mom of a special-needs child, I have to say that there are a ton of moms like me who would latch onto Patty and what she knows. Then we wouldn't feel as if we're the only mom on the planet who some days wishes her kid was average and some days wishes it wasn't so hard.

So don't think you aren't an expert. Don't question your value. Don't question what expertise you have, because I promise that you are a gold mine and a treasure trove of information; you just have to find a way to share it.

Is everybody convinced that you're an expert? Pick up your pen and scrawl on this page what you're an expert in. Don't think too hard—just write. (If you have expertise in any of the following areas, just circle those.)

fitness	coaching
software applications	hair
business optimization	real estate
flying	autism
homeschooling	health
single moms raising teenage kids	frugality
special education	writing
quilting	accounting
home birth	speaking/teaching/preaching
gardening	parenting
home repair	lawn care
typing/word processing	law
video	

What is your expertise? It might not be listed above—it has to come from *you*! That is the freedom (and perhaps the curse) of being your own boss, of creating a home-based business—the fact that there are really no rules, no mold, no exact template. This is about *you* and the special gifts you bring to the table.

I found that reading Max Lucado's *Cure for the Common Life* was a huge eye-opener for me. Going through the exercises he outlines in his book helped me really "get" what I'm about and how I can be serving better and playing bigger.

Now that you're convinced you're an expert and you know who you want to serve and you're brainstorming those models and *how* you're going to serve them, let's move forward and talk about where they'll find you, where you'll find them, and how to connect you to your ideal market.

Eighteen

Ideas to Income

Selling to people who actually want to hear from you is more effective than interrupting strangers who don't.

—Seth Godin

Maybe you're stuck in your idea and you're confused by all the strategies. You want to know how to get from idea to income. So if you are now asking, "How do I get it out of my head or off my hard drive and turn it into an income opportunity?" then this chapter is for you.

Don't think this is going to be complicated. It is not. Part of the issue is that many of us are overcomplicating things.

Getting Past the Excuses

I want to walk you through some of the processes I use. Number one, how to weed out some of the unnecessary ideas—the things that aren't necessarily going to be profitable for you—how to eliminate the overwhelming things, and how to focus on what is really important.

You might be tempted to cross your arms and say, "Well, but—"

I'll say this just once—if you are going to succeed in business, you need to get off your "but" and find solutions instead of excuses. I can help you with that. Just quit telling me all the reasons this isn't going to work. My admonition to you is that you don't just read this but that you read, take notes, and immediately apply something that you're learning.

Some of you who are more advanced are going to say, "Oh, well, I already know all of this. I'm already great at all of this." Super. Read anyway. It might just be for that one idea.

I was with Zig Ziglar recently and he let me know that even at eighty-four, he still reads three hours a day. He's "been there and done that" with his career. We all know his name. We're all familiar with Zig in the business and personal self-growth industry. He reads books that you wouldn't imagine that he reads. He says he reads everything but fiction and that he reads for that one idea, that one improvement, that one encouragement, that one resource, or that one connection.

Today I'm encouraging you to read for that one idea or prompt that will move you into action. I don't mean that one idea about a new product or service. I mean the idea about how to improve what you're already doing.

With entrepreneurs the problem is not a lack of ideas, is it? The problem is typically too many ideas, too many bright shiny objects, too many directions we can get excited about, and too many things in our lives that we need to be focused on. Am I right? Are you nodding your head? So it isn't lack of ideas but what to do with all those great ideas.

I've found my own 'Escape Velocity'—my own sense of doing what it is I want to do, and I'm most definitely working in the world that I want to be working in. That's why I feel a sense of overnight success, finally, after twelve years of pushing harder and harder.

Success, you see, isn't a mansion and a yacht. Success is living the life you want and doing the work you're best at doing with the people you know will help you reach the next level. Success means working on projects that you know will fulfill a deep-felt passion within you and yet will feed your family. Success is knowing that you've built a thriving network of people who all work hard to grow each other's capabilities. Success means finding a next angle and vectoring your efforts toward growing that out. Success means having the means and capability to make better decisions. Success means getting home in time for dinner. Success means leaving the house when I want to and staying home with the kids when I want to, all while making a future for my family.

—*Chris Brogan, best-selling author*

You need to have a journal or an idea book. I recommend that it not be electronic—in your phone or your Palm or computer. I have a small notebook that I keep in my purse and a bigger notebook that I carry to business meetings. I have *idea* pages—you need to write those ideas down as soon as you think of them. You don't need to implement them as soon as you think of them, but you do need to write them down. Our memories are short and the moment will pass. The root of the word *inspired* means "God-breathed." If they're really divine moments of inspiration, you don't want to check back and try to rack your brain about it later. It might be gone.

Here is an example. I'm a big fan of the books *The Go-Giver* and *Go-Givers Sell More*. One of the coauthors, Bob Burg, hosted an event in Orlando I attended last weekend.

I woke up one morning with a book title in my head: *Go-Giver Kids*. I wrote it down, put it in my phone, and e-mailed Bob and told him I had an idea I wanted to talk about when I got to the event. As soon as I saw him I said, "Before you even say hello or you're glad I'm here, listen. You need to write *Go-Giver Kids*. You need to write this as a parable for kids because parents are going to be quick to acknowledge that their kids need help being better siblings, better community members, and better students, and the kids can then teach their parents." Go-Giver Kids—okay, whew! I felt better. I gave him that idea and then I let it go.

It didn't have to be an idea for me. How could I morph Go-Giver Kids into something in my business? How could I market that idea? But it was an idea that someone needed to act on. I wrote it down specifically for Bob and then I got it off my brain. You need to do the same thing with every idea you have. You need to honor those ideas. Put them in your journal.

Put a little star by it if the idea is related to your current profitable business, and if it isn't—if it's random—then set it aside and revisit it later. If it does not fit in your current core model, then you might need to save it for when you have a lot of downtime and can do something just for fun. Or you might say: "Oh, that's awesome! That's an awesome idea. Let me call Bob. That fits into his business model."

"Well, now, Carrie, I don't know. I don't know if I want to give away my ideas. They're good and profitable ideas."

Okay, you can put your idea on eBay and see if anybody buys it or you can give it to somebody in your network and let him be grateful and proud of what he does with it, and know that someone at another time is going to have a rock-star idea for you.

I'm never out of ideas, and I get some of the best ideas from other people. When you can give an idea to somebody else, you can cross it off your list. Then you don't nag until he does something with it—it is his responsibility. It's a gift you've given to someone.

I usually like to sit on my ideas in my journal for a little while. Sometimes I'll come back to them three weeks later or even three months later and say: "Oh, wow. That idea I was really hot about makes absolutely no sense in my model right now" or "I just don't see where I can develop that without a lot of time, money, and energy. It's not a fit for me right now." Then I cross it off.

It's dangerous to be chasing every little idea, but some of those ideas will be great for other people. I always write ideas down. After I review an idea, sometimes I think, *This is really an idea I need to pursue.* Then that idea goes on a smaller list. I follow this process every time.

Qualifying Your Ideas

What is your motive in your business right now? What is your primary motive? When you're qualifying your ideas:

1. Honor the idea by writing it down.
2. Give it some time and let it "marinate."
3. Ask: What is my motive for my business right now? You're going to put it through the motive filter.

You might think your motive for business is always money—not necessarily. Your primary motive in your business right now could be list building or lead generation.

- Is your primary motive cash generation?
- Is your primary motive credibility building and platform building?
- Is your primary motive product creation?

Motives for business tend to fall into those categories.

Or is your primary motive to get from offline to online but with the same business?

Laurie Taylor has a really great offline business. She's with IgniteYourBiz.com and her primary motive is to get from offline to online and be more streamlined and convert things little by little. So she will filter her ideas and new project thoughts based on her motives, which are not cash first but online systems.

What is your primary motive? Write that above your idea. Always remember what your primary motive and your secondary motive are. Let's say your primary motive is lead generation—you need more names on your e-mail list, more prospects in your Rolodex, or more potential face-to-face sales appointments—and your secondary motive is cash. Then when you're looking at your list of five to ten ideas, you do a one to ten rating or one to four, or however you want to rate them. For example:

Widget Idea #1—How well does this meet your number one objective of lead generation?

1. Not at all
2. Kind of
3. Strongly
4. Absolutely

Don't overthink it. Go with your gut. Then you can come back in a second column and ask, "Now, how much does this meet the secondary objective of cash?"

The third column I like to do is just bottom-line cash numbers. How many leads could this potentially generate in the next thirty days if I just buckled down and put on my blinders and really focused? How much could this really generate for me lead-wise? Your primary motive is leads—how many leads? Then in thirty days how much cash would this generate? If you're looking at thirty days of focus or looking at a forty-day focus period, how much would this meet your objectives of lead and cash generation?

Then you rank them in descending order of your primary and secondary objective average—meaning maybe idea number three would bring you the most leads with the least cash. Maybe idea number four brings you to fewer leads than number three but a lot of cash. This is why knowing your motives and priorities is important so you can be somewhat objective about what to pursue, always going back to the question, "Does this meet my primary business motive right now?"

Average it out and see which idea meets both of your objectives well and focus on that one idea first. If you're like me, you will have little scribbles and lists and arrows all over this chart. That's good. Sometimes we just go, "Oh, there's a killing there. I'm sitting on a gold mine."

I really hate the phrase "sitting on a gold mine" because it overwhelms people. *Acccck!* What am I doing wrong that I can't tap the gold mine? That's so much pressure. I think everyone is sitting on a gold mine; it's just a matter of chipping away at the right spots to get to where we want to be.

On a monthly basis I revisit this process with what I'm currently working on. Yesterday was that day for me. I'll be really open with you—I reevaluated some big core things I'm working on, and guess what? Some of the things that were so important to me six months ago are not as important to me now. They don't meet my current objectives—my objectives have changed. My objectives are not list building or cash building. My objectives are moving into a different arena in some of my core focuses. I don't mean to be vague, but I don't want to taint what you're thinking about your business.

As you start meeting your cash goals and your lead goals, you will have the luxury of moving into some other objectives. Then you have to look back at your core businesses and ask, "Okay, now how are my core businesses meeting my objectives? How can we get them to meet the objectives? How can we focus differently?" This should be a very eye-opening experience for you.

Did any of this have to do with technology or strategy or avoiding being overwhelmed? No. We're still in the idea phase.

Now you have your ideas narrowed down. Let's say you're going to take your one core focus idea. On coaching calls I say over and over: "You have to focus. What are you focused on? That's a great idea, but how does it work into your current focus?" My clients get frustrated with me. Yes, I'm saying the same thing over and over. There's a reason for that. I want you to know that I'm just looking out for your best interests. You have to look at your motives and objectives and whether or not they fit into your business model.

Just because something is a good idea does not mean you have to do it. Sometimes it means saying no to good ideas in order to embrace the really great opportunities. If you're too busy with the good stuff, you never have room for the great stuff. Keep that in mind. I have to say no to a lot of opportunities, and some of those may be things you've asked me to do. I have to say no to some invitations to be places that would be good places to be, but freeing that up allows me to do some great stuff.

Yesterday in the process of reevaluating some major things and making some huge decisions, I took a big step and made a big shift in one area. Literally within two hours, I had another opportunity open up that was such a blessing that I might have been too overwhelmed to think of four or five hours before. It never ceases to amaze me how when you are really disciplined about saying no and walking away from some things that might be good or helpful or have some good long-term potential, it leaves room for some great stuff. I want you to keep that in mind.

After you get your core idea, I want you to write down what you perceive as a timeline on this. How quickly could you get this to market? Put a date as your timeline. I like a specific date instead of a vague "three weeks." It's more of a commitment.

Then back it up and ask, "What do I perceive as some obstacles?" Write *obstacles* really big. Let's just go ahead and pull those out. They're lurking there. You're already saying, "But, oh, but . . . but . . . but—" So let's get off your "buts" and write them down. What are your obstacles?

"Well, May is such a busy month in school with the kids." Yes, it is. You should see my calendar! "Technology totally overwhelms me and this is going to require some online stuff. I don't have the money to invest in this." Write down your obstacles.

Your Turn

You've already done the objective on this exercise. You're going to focus on the idea. What's the timeline? What are the three biggest obstacles you can perceive? Write those down right now.

Idea:

_____

_____

Timeline:

_____

_____

Obstacles:

_____

_____

_____

_____

_____

_____

Did you write down those major obstacles? Good. Now go down to another line and write down the three most positive benefits.

_____

_____

_____

On one end you're saying why it won't work and what's going to get between you and this. On the other end you're going to talk about the three most positive benefits.

What was easier—to write down your obstacles or to write down the benefits? Was it easier to list your obstacles or easier to list the benefits? Did you struggle with that at all?

Keep this piece of paper in front of you when you're working on the idea. Now next to the obstacles, put an arrow down the page—for obstacles one, two, and three. Right next to them put how you can prevent them or head them off. You already see them coming, so what can you do to take a detour?

If you follow me on Twitter, I've said, "A disappointment is not a stop sign in your journey. It's a 'detour sign'—a 'go a different route' sign. If we already know that this is the bridge that I think is going to be out on my journey, this is the plane that's going to be grounded because of the volcano on my journey, what plan can you make ahead of time to prevent that from happening?"

This is the core strategy in my business. This is one of the most important things that you can learn from me. Since I can't sit in the room with each of you and make you do this, I want to lead you through this right now. Uncross your arms and start doing some chicken scratch. You will find this helpful. You will find this super helpful. I want you to go back to where your obstacles are and start writing how you can prevent those obstacles from happening.

If you wrote down, "I'm just aware it's going to happen, so it won't really happen" or "I just won't get too busy and I'll plan things out"—that's not specific enough. You need to be really specific on this. If you know that you'll have roadblocks from the kids' schedule this month or the publishing schedule or from your real job, or if you know of another issue, then you need to put specific strategies in place. I want you to be really specific on these. Now let's move to the benefits.

You might have put "more money so I can pay my bills or won't be so stressed-out"—or whatever. You need some really specific benefits. Things like "I can send so-and-so to camp, pay off such-and-such credit cards," whatever the exact benefit is. You need to be very specific.

Underneath that I need you to answer this question—write it down so you can remember—"What's so great about that?" Next to your benefits of focusing on this one idea I need you to specifically say what they are. Assign numbers or dates or whatever you need to do—be very specific and answer this question: "What's so great about that?" This question is for each of the benefits you've listed. Don't skip over this. It's your "why."

This is what's going to propel you through the next thirty days. Thirty days from now, you are going to have accomplished the things on your list if you stick to your focus. Go ahead and be specific right now. The more concrete you are with these benefits, then the more committed you tend to be to taking the action leading up to the benefits.

Being Accountable for Success

When I started the Barefoot Executive, I already had another business offline—a busy and lucrative business. I had a newborn, a three-year-old, and the other two kids were preteens. I said to my husband and kids, "I'm going to start a new something. I just don't know exactly how it's all going to look, but I have some ideas and I'm asking for six months to prove this model. I'm asking for six months of your sacrificing a little time with me, your being patient with me.

"Here's what the benefits are going to be—eventually it will be a new model for Mom (me) that will be a little more forgiving time-wise, a little more virtual, and I really think this is going to be a good move. But here's the benefit for you—I chose a vacation at Beaches.com. The

Sesame Street characters live there. This is where we're going to go in six months. We're going to pay cash for this from Mom's new business. We're not going to take the laptop or cell phone, and it's going to be all about you all week long. It's going to be so much fun."

Then we watched the Beaches.com video online every single day. We had a poster up so they could focus on it. That helped us focus. It was a very concrete benefit with a date and a price tag. (If you want to be held accountable, then you tell your three-year-old what you're promising.)

You need to be as specific as possible. You need to be accountable to your family—and a peer group is even better. You need to be accountable to a business partner. What do you need to be accountable for? You need to be accountable for concrete goals with deadlines and measurable numbers. You may be hesitating about writing these down. Here's why—it's easier to let yourself off the hook when you haven't committed on paper. Again, we haven't gotten into technology or strategies or social media or SEO (search engine optimization). That's all noise. It's about your idea and about the income or end result of time, money, and what's going on.

What's in between the idea and the income? You heard this in geometry class. You've heard this all your life: "The shortest distance between two points is a straight line." Sometimes that line zigs and zags—I'll be honest with you. That's why we're overcoming those obstacles early. I'd rather be able to anticipate the obstacles and follow the zig and the zag than to feel as if I have to give up every time.

The Implementation

In order to take this idea to income, ask, "What are five key steps I need to take? What are five core actions I need to take?" Is it to make an audio recording? Is it to write a chapter? Is it to set up a teleclass? Is it talk to so-and-so about helping me with content? This is the implementation. What are five steps you need to take? "Tech stuff" is not an entire step. You need to break that down into five key steps. Write them yourself.

Five Key Steps

1. _____

2. _____

3. _____

4. _____

5. _____

How did that feel? Are you being specific enough? Are you being detailed enough? You may be saying you don't know five steps. Okay, do you know the first step? Do you know the first thing you think needs to be done? Do you know one of the close-to-the-end steps? Write those down.

Then ask yourself, *What am I missing? What are the gaps?*

I believe this is an amazing process. This is something you can do over and over again.

It's true. With every idea, every phase of your journey, and every tweak of a new thing, you need to stop and go through the process. It's really helpful. Many of us who flew by the seat of our pants before and then started implementing this, now say, "Wow! This process sure saves me a lot of time, energy, money, mistakes, and frustration when things go wrong." And guess what? They will (go wrong).

What It Looks Like

Need some examples of key steps? Let's say my idea is publishing a book. That's a big one. You could substitute in here publishing an e-book, doing an audio, doing a teleclass. That could be your big idea for your market or your niche. What would be my key steps for publishing a book? One—I need to decide if I'm going to self-publish or publish with a publishing house. Will it be electronic? That might need to be in my obstacle/benefits part, but the key steps would be:

1. Identify my title and create a table of contents.
2. Set aside daily time to write—one hour a day.
3. Interview A, B, C people for chapters of my book. Of course, that depends on the idea and the format of my book.
4. Have a cover designed and some graphics created.
5. Set up an account with a self-publisher or secure the contact information of some literary agents to whom I can forward the manuscript.

You just have to break it down.

Even when my schedule, my deadlines, and my business aren't easy, I'm passionate about the results for my family and passionate about the change in my business. I'm passionate about the people I work with and it keeps me moving forward even though it's sometimes difficult.

I can't tell you how to make yourself serious about your business. I can't inspire you or motivate you. I can't move you to action. Only you can do it, but you have to want it. You have to want it, period.

We've gone from ideas to the benefits, the income, and the end result. We've backed up into implementation. Now the really important thing about your five key steps of implementation is that it lessens what overwhelms you from A to Z. It helps you break down the little things—knowing what the obstacles may be—knowing what you're going to overcome. You can head those off at the pass. Then you can also see what can be delegated, what can be outsourced or bartered, and what you really need to do yourself.

Write dates next to your five steps of implementation. You already have an end date for your benefits. Back up and see what dates you need to do those steps to meet that end date. When do you need to have each step finished? Assign a specific date. This gives you a road map that drives you on the path from idea to income.

Along the way you have the implementation. Too many times we have the idea and that's where we stop. I've said before that an idea is just an idea until you take action. When you implement an idea, you can turn it into income. That is the magic formula in business. The faster you make the middle part happen, the faster you'll experience those powerful, energy-giving benefits. I think you can see how this process is going to clarify a lot about your business.

"Carrie, how do I know what to focus on?"
"Carrie, how do I know if this is going to meet my objectives?"
"Carrie, I'm so overwhelmed with what to do next."

We just solved all of those problems. Before you move to idea number two or idea number eight or number seven, go back and repeat the process again.

It doesn't have to be overwhelming. It isn't unachievable. This is your framework. This is like the shampoo bottle instructions: lather, rinse, repeat. It's just that simple. (Not always easy, but it can be simple.)

Why are you still reading? You have work to do, right?

Quite honestly, this is a chapter you can revisit over and over again with every new product, service, or opportunity. Funnel your ideas through this process and revaluate what you're doing and what your action steps are. Put dates by these steps, then commit. Once you really, really commit, things will line up, and obstacles won't seem like such a big deal.

In the spring of 2010, I was stuck in Ireland on a business-trip-turned-vacation due to the Icelandic volcano that spewed ash into the atmosphere and stopped international air travel. I needed to get to Orlando to speak. I had committed to be there for my friends and hosts Thom Scott and Bob Burg. Through a series of events and actions and processes, we made it happen.

I was on the ground in Dallas less than twelve hours, including the drive to and from the airport to switch out suitcases and briefly kiss my little ones, whom I had been away from for almost two weeks now because of the weather calamity. I had a serious case of "Momflict," and I know that no one would have condemned me for missing that event.

Long story short (if possible), I shared the stage with a speaker who not only proved to be valuable for my audience but also led me to a personal relationship with a longtime hero and mentor of mine, whom I can now call a colleague and associate. Because I made a commitment, I had a weekend that quite possibly has altered the direction of my business growth and life.

You have to know your "why"—what drives you. You have to commit, no outs, no excuses.

So focus on this I-to-I process right now. It is all about taking your ideas to income by following the road of implementation.

Nineteen

Where Will They Find You?

Exposure plus ninety-five cents might buy you a decent cup of coffee. The key is to "position" yourself in your market as the expert, the resource, the only person your prospect would ever even think of doing business with, or referring to others.

—Bob Burg

Can Your Customers Find You?

Where will you set up shop?
Are you visible?
What is a first step?

In my work as a representative for Google, Inc., to small business owners everywhere, our core message is: if you are not online, you are invisible.

The world has shifted. We've moved from the streets and the corners the interconnected space online known as the World Wide Web. This is news. You've seen the transition. You are talking to your friends and fily on Facebook, you are reading (or maybe even writing) a blog, and might even look for deals, sales, movie times, or maps online. These si

things seem—well, simple. But the fact is, business has made a major shift and as a small business owner, you need to be aware of a few things.

According to webpronews.com, more than half of all consumers begin their purchasing decisions online. This is regardless of whether the product, service, or commodity is available online. The research, the reputation, and the contact information—these are things your potential customer is looking for. And guess what? If they don't find you when they are looking—you are invisible. You don't exist. They cannot purchase from you if you don't pop up into their range of vision.

Extreme statement? Perhaps! But yellow pages are phasing out and traditional methods of direct response such as billboards, television ads, and radio spots are directing prospects to Web pages and online resources.

What's a small business to do?

Be found. Be online. Be visible. Be effective.

It's a new world of business, and it is no longer enough to have happy customers, a visible storefront, and local newspaper advertising. You must have "online real estate" as well.

Another fact to keep in mind is that your prospects are not necessarily searching for you by name but by location, by reputation, and also by the problem that you could solve for them. This can all be very intimidating, right?

A few questions or thoughts that might immediately pop into your head:

"I can't afford a fancy Web site."

"I don't know anything about technical stuff or computers."

"I have an established business; I don't need to be online."

"I am already so busy; when can I fit in something extra?"

"I don't think my customers use the Internet."

"I don't want to sell online."

"I've tried that before [or have a friend who did], and it didn't work."

Those are all valid points and we'll talk a bit about each of those objections. I won't concede on one point, however. You must be online. *Must.* Nonnegotiable.

A Web site/Web space has gone beyond being an "extra" or a "luxury" in business to being an absolute necessity. Keep reading and you'll see why.

What Is Online Marketing?

There is a myth, a common misconception, that online marketing is a business model, a new trend in doing business, an either/or to business. I disagree.

I think business is business is business. Some businesses have a store. Some have an office. Some operate from home. Some operate "on the go." But having a profitable business means you have an in-demand product or service that meets customer needs in exchange for money. Right? The fulfillment is not an issue. I am imagining conversations from years ago:

"This talking radio won't last. It will be a flash in the pan. I can't imagine why companies would spend money for these things called commercials. Throwing money away is what that is. I don't want to be in 'radio marketing,' I just want to do business. Word of mouth was good enough for my grandparents' general store, and it's good enough for me."

"These newspaper rags—people don't read those for ads and sales. They trust their friends, not some paid placement. I refuse to be labeled a 'newspaper marketer,' and I won't participate (*grumble, grumble*)."

"These kids today think that being a 'billboard marketer' or 'direct mail marketer' or 'yellow pages marketer' is going to bring them customers and store awareness. Silliness, all of it. Business is business. Just let me work. I'm too busy to bother with all of that anyway."

"This 'television box' is a trend. I'm not going to spend any money advertising on that. I don't want to be a 'TV marketer.'"

Do you see where I'm going? We know that marketing—using the available tools, techniques, and technology—has been a must for business since the dawn of commerce, yet we still fight every new strategy as it comes along.

You need to consider a Web presence as necessary as a sign in your window, your Better Business Bureau registration, your bank account, and your business card. It's a must.

Quite simply, online marketing is utilizing the Internet—the World Wide Web—to get information about you—your products, services, storefront, location, hours, and your unique selling proposition—out into the world. There is nothing trendy, risky, or optional about it anymore.

It's not for the *elite*—it's for the *enlightened*.

What Is Your Ultimate Goal with a Web Presence?

What do you want to get out of being online? I believe that in every new endeavor or every adoption of something new in your business, you need to know your motives. Here are a few that might be on your mind.

- Do you want new customers?
- Do you want to broadcast store location and hours?
- Do you want previous customers to remember you?
- Do you want to showcase clients' testimonials or praise?
- Do you want to establish trust and credibility with information about you, the owner?
- Do you want to showcase specials or offers?
- Do you want to highlight your community or your charity involvement?
- Do you want to increase traffic on slow days?

These motives are all very valid and very possible to accomplish. You can do all of these with a simple Web page. Critics might say, "So what? I have a Web page and everyone knows that the average Web surfer only gives you ten seconds before they decide if you're worthwhile or not."

Maybe that's true. But if they don't find you at all because you're not online, you don't even get those ten seconds. And if you can utilize this book to maximize your impact in those ten seconds, then you can turn that into ten dollars, ten sales, ten appointments, ten customers, or ten referrals. That certainly is worth further investigation, right?

How Can You Tell If Your Online Marketing Is Effective?

This is a bit difficult to gauge at first, so instead of specific tracking at this stage of the game, let me give you some suggestions on saturation. Before you get the response you want or need, you have to do a bit of saturation.

- Print your site on customer receipts and add it to your e-mail signatures.
- Always include your Web presence on customer mailings.
- Send customers online with any traditional advertising you do.
- Have your Web site on your company vehicles, containers, bags, materials, and so forth.
- Point folks to your site through your presence in social media.

"Carrie, isn't that redundant? That seems like I'm nagging or repeating myself." Great question! But saturating your market and your materials will help you get an incredible contagious word of mouth going. You will be surprised at how many folks will come to your page who wouldn't have known about it otherwise. This is just one step, however. We will also talk about aggressively finding *new* folks online and attracting them to you.

But first—you must *be* present online. You must. None of the rest of this book will work or make sense if you don't embrace this truth as your own.

Checklist—Start Now

This one is almost too easy. Get your Google Places page or list yourself in online registries. Many of these are free and have online tutorials for signing up. Go to your Web search tool and type in "business registry for_____." In that blank you want to put your business type for more targeted results.

The important thing is that you just *start*. Get your business name, geographical area, hours, phone and *show up* online. This is your first step to recovering from "Web invisibility."

205

If you already have some sort of Web site or blog, then I suggest adding the following:

- A customer photo or video with a testimonial or "rave" about your company (You can also do this on your social media networks like Twitter, Facebook, YouTube, and LinkedIn.)
- Photos of current product, storefront, or team members serving happy customers
- Audio or video of *you* welcoming customers or giving them some information about your business

I admit—this might seem too simplistic to you. But we're establishing trust and presence. No need to get overcomplicated.

Another *must* that we will discuss in the following chapters is collecting prospects' names and e-mail addresses. Phone numbers and mailing addresses are not enough anymore. Add an opt-in form or an incentive for customers to leave their names and e-mail addresses. Perhaps you have specials you will announce or tips and tricks you'll share.

Set up an e-mail service account with MailChimp, Aweber, or Constant Contact so that you can keep in touch with your customers on a regular basis. (This really could be an entire chapter in itself, but you can find some tutorials and resources at BarefootExecutiveResources.com.)

Offer an incentive for clients and customers to leave feedback, testimonials, and suggestions on your site, blog, or social media networks.

Check and double-check that your site is everywhere—on receipts, printed materials, signs, advertisements—*everywhere*. (I cannot emphasize this enough.)

Now you are really ready to get started, to increase your visibility and your traction in the marketplace, whether you are looking for world domination or just a few hundred dollars a month.

Twenty

Building Your Audience

The goal of an effective sales process is to get rid of bad fits as quickly as you can, so that you can continue to fill your sales funnel with more qualified prospects.

—Pamela Slim, *Escape from Cubicle Nation*

In this chapter we are going to talk a little bit about filling your stadium.

I have three core businesses offline and online. I've done service business, merchandising business, and sales businesses. I've taught. I've done corporate America. You know, I've done it all. I will never be Miss America. I'm good with that. I am, however, "Miss Ellaneous," so that qualifies me to be me.

Here's just a little bit of my online story. We are going to talk about building your stadium, building your audience first. I like to say that what I do is the reverse Ziglar method. I didn't start with a little bit here and a little bit there and build bigger and bigger and bigger to be a legend. I decided to start the standing ovation before I even got to the stage.

In your business, what if your store was full before you ever opened the doors? What if you were an independent film producer and the theater was full before you finished producing the movie? Have you heard stories about people who so believe in their movie that they mortgage their house and sell their plasma and do all sorts of things and then they produce the movie, and guess who is there to watch it? Mom, Dad, and Uncle Herman, who wanted to get in free because he's sure not paying because he's Uncle Herman. And so it flopped, they are out all the money, and nobody even saw the movie.

Well, what if instead you filled the theater to capacity and then you find out what these like-minded people want to see and hear and know? And then what if you serve them popcorn and sell them candy and soft drinks while they are waiting? And then you deliver the experience that they've chosen. Does that sound like a better way to do business? It's kind of a reverse mind-set, isn't it? It's hard. Online they call it *list building* and offline they call it *lead generation*. I call it *filling your stadium*. I've been online just at two and a half years now. I got Internet Marketer of the Year when I had been online about fourteen months. We did six figures online our first ten months. Again, this is in addition to my other companies, so this was a part-time venture with four kids. I started online when I had a ten-week-old.

So, that's what I know. I have one hundred thousand subscribers to my e-mail list, my social media list, my YouTube channel, my Barefoot Executive TV, and my Facebook Fan Page.

I know a few things about building your fan base. By using some of the strategies that we've put in place online and offline and through actual networking, you can have that many people ready to listen to you, ready to get to know you, or at least just curious. Curiosity marketing is the best thing ever.

You can implement these things. In less than two and a half years, we have built a seven-figure presence in our businesses online with more than one hundred thousand followers. I turn down way more speaking engagements than I accept. I'm mentoring with Zig Ziglar and Dr. John Maxwell. These opportunities would not have been available to me two years ago. Do you see that? This is a by-product of filling my stadium.

You know you have a great product. You know you have a great service. You know your book is amazing, you know your program is this, you know your service is that, you know your dry cleaner is the best, you know your wedding planning service is the best, your coaching is outstanding. You are a rock star, a great speaker, or maybe you are a great musician and your music needs to be heard. Whatever it is, don't cross your arms and say to me, "My business is different." Hogwash. Business is business.

The truth is that when we create something, our people are such fans and our audience is so dedicated that if it has the brand name on it, they buy it. They love it. We have an audience waiting. So then the only thing that remains is to grow your audience. Grow the number of people listening.

Anybody heard of Justin Bieber? Justin Bieber built up his audience before he got a record label. Anybody know how he did that? He had these YouTube videos of him singing. He started his career by sharing his music on YouTube. He built up a fan base on social media and YouTube, and the rest is history. His music started with a huge fan base and *then* was monetized into a business.

If it applies to music and it applies to business, then it applies to authors with their books too. You can see that if I take something to a huge crowd of folks who have assembled themselves, I don't have to survey them, I don't have to wonder or overanalyze or whatever because even if 10 percent of these people buy what I have, that's still good. Right?

Justin Bieber did not have to spend years building up his audience or sweating in nightclubs. Good thing, because he's not old enough. But he now plays to audiences of thousands, sells thousands of recordings, and has even written the story of his life so far.

Want Them

Do you really want these people in your audience? Why is that? What's so great about these people? Am I helping you realize that it can be done? It doesn't have to look the same as somebody else's dream. It doesn't have to look the same as somebody else's business model. It doesn't have to look the same as what you were brought up with.

You have to really want these people in your stadium. Why do you want them? "Oh, it's just about the money." "Oh, this is the best market." You have to really want them, but why? You have to be really clear on your "why," and you have to want Franklin and Daisy and Jay and not just numbers upon numbers upon numbers.

Yes, I believe there are good things that come in the numbers because that enables me to meet and know more of you. I care about the people I do business with. Do you care about the end result for your clients? What are you solving for them?

Do you care about these people? Why do you want them? People have a radar, a very intense radar of mistrust, and they can spot insincerity. Can't you? We are programmed that way.

Woo Them

If you want them, then you need to woo them. I use a series of techniques—online list building, offline networking, and even an automated greeting card system called Send Out Cards. Seriously, it's a good system to help you follow up with people, connect with people, send pictures of yourself with people. You need to be wooing them. You also can do this online with lead pages—"squeeze pages." You've seen the forms that ask for your name and e-mail? That's a squeeze page. That's a list builder page, a lead generation page. You don't want the immediate sale, contrary to what you might think. What you want is their name and their e-mail.

If they are giving you three seconds on your Web page and they see the form requesting name and e-mail versus a sales pitch, what are they conditioned to do? I hope you answered, "Fill it in" because the subconscious mind is programmed to fill in blanks and follow instructions.

Truthfully, your ideal target audience wants you to woo them. People want to be romanced—not just women, men too. What does that mean?

I sent out a video recently called *Sensuality Marketing*. People say, "Ooh, sensuality marketing? She said she was a preacher's kid." Okay, the root word of *sensuality* is what? *Sense*. How many senses do you have? You have five senses—*five* senses. You need to market with all of those senses. If you only have three seconds, not a lot of wooing and romance can go on there.

You have to build a relationship. You cannot build a relationship in three seconds or three minutes. You need their names and their e-mail addresses. This is why I consistently excel in the businesses I pursue. It's because I'm building relationships with people. It's not about who you know. It's not about what you know. It's not even about who knows you. It's about who *feels* like they know you.

You've got to be open with people and honest with people. You may not have to be quite as honest as I am, but you have to let people feel like they are in with you. That's part of the wooing process—good information, good content, good videos, good social media. That's all part of the process.

Win Them

You need to want them, you need to woo them, and then you need to win them. Does this sound like the dating process? But it continues. You need to win them, and win them again. You need to win them by presenting them with solid products, services, and offers—even if they are not ones that you personally provide but ones that somebody else in your circle provides.

- Do you know—really, really know—without a shadow of a doubt that you have a rock-solid product?
- Do you know without a shadow of a doubt you are a rock-solid, rock-star coach and you can offer results?
- Do you provide an amazing service?
- Do you know your book is amazing and could change people's lives if they would read it and make a decision?
- Do you know that you are a good speaker—you just need more stages?

More people need to know, right? So you have to tell them and you have to make them offers. Now, this is another conundrum in the marketing space. Some people are good list builders, but then they never make offers to their list because they say, "I don't want them to feel like I'm being too salesy." That's what lists are for. If you take me out on a date and then date two and date three and you never hold my hand or kiss me, I'm going to start getting a complex. Right?

Why isn't he delivering on what I suspected he had to offer? He sure talked a good game before we started going out. Now he won't even hold my hand. You've got to win them. You've got to make offers. You have to let them know you believe in your business. If you are apologizing for selling something, you are apologizing for being in business, so you don't need to be in business. Go get a job. My friend Steve Kloyda says, "If you knew the cure to cancer and you knew fifteen people who had cancer or whose loved ones had cancer—how long would it take you to get on the phone?"

Seconds, right? It would literally take you seconds to dial the phone. And then, would you apologize? "I'm sorry to bother you. I'm sorry to tell you, but I found the cure to cancer and I don't want you to think I am selling anything." They would not care what that doctor charged. They would not care. They would want to know. If you have the answer to somebody's problem, tell him.

Business boils down to three points. This is million-dollar advice right here.

- Build your list. Fill your stadium, essentially.
- Make an offer.
- Repeat. Keep building your list. Keep filling your funnel. Keep making offers.

Now, in between there, you can ask, "Oh, but do I create a product, do I write a book, do I become a speaker, do I become a coach? What do I do?" That's just the vehicle in which you are delivering it. It's inconsequential. You have to have prospects and you have to have profits.

Wow Them

Once you get their business, then you need to wow them. What do I mean by that? Over and over again, give more than they expect. Deliver more content than they expect.

BarefootExecutive.TV is one of my wow factors. It's my own online network where I deliver free three- to eight-minute business episodes on a regular basis. I have it professionally produced and I don't charge for it. Why would I do that? Because I want my clients to feel like they know me. I want them to know that I'm in their brains. I know what they are thinking about. I get a huge volume of e-mails. "Carrie, are you reading my mind? How did you know I needed that episode today?" I wow them over and over, or at least I try to.

That brings me to another point. You cannot control the results. You can only control your efforts.

Deliver over and over again. People love to laugh. People love for you to touch their emotions. You can't control whether they laugh, and you can't control whether you touch their emotions; you can't control whether they buy, but you can set up the right scenarios if you really, really want them. The Barefoot Community, the people that I hang out with, the people on my list and in my audience, I love them and they know that. That's why they stay. That's why they work with me.

My friend Craig Ballantyne is dumbfounded by the connection I have with my audience. He said to me, "They just adore you." I said, "You know what? It's not that they adore me, it's that they adore the fact that they know I adore them."

You have to want them; you have to woo them. This is when you are building your list. Then you win them with good content, good courses. I hear this a lot: "Am I giving too much away?" "Am I teaching too much for free?" Not possible.

You want to win them with good content, great stories, and filler; and then you want to wow them over and over—over-deliver on the course. If you ask, "What can I deliver at what price point and just be enough so that I'm not working too hard?" that is the wrong mind-set. That's not how you are going to fill your stadium.

Twenty-one

Where Will You Find Them?

We get paid for bringing value to the market place.

—Jim Rohn

You cannot sell to an empty stadium. You cannot sell to an empty room. And so a lot of what I want to talk about is always making sure you have someone to sell your products, services, or offerings to.

If you always have an audience, people listening, people who have already raised their hands and said, "Yes, I want to be in your space. Yes, I have a relationship with you. Yes, let's do business," then that makes your job so much easier.

In addition to filling your own stadium, why not do what sports teams have been doing for years—leveraging other people's stadiums? Let's see who else is serving the market that you want to serve.

Finding Them Offline

Where will you find them? Who else has access to them?

Don't forget live events, live networking, and live connections. This might be a local chamber of commerce meeting, a meet up, a Tweetup, a seminar, a class—whatever you need to do to meet people for real.

You can't do everything online. You can't do everything by mail and on the phone. You can, but you are going to limit your effectiveness.

Some of the best relationships you will have begin online and then may be cemented in person, or vice versa. You need a multifaceted approach. Don't think just because you are doing some online things you can totally give up on the chamber of commerce or meeting people at live industry-related events.

Your Turn

What are some live events that are available to you?

_____

_____

_____

_____

Some of my favorite strategies for live events:

- Taking pictures of people I meet
- Researching and going with a "hit" list; who are the speakers going to be? Who else is going to be there? It helps to have a little bit of info before you get there.
- Going with the attitude of service. How can I serve these people, not what can I sell to these people? Some of these people are uncertain, unsure of themselves, and have low self-esteem. How can I serve them? How can I make them feel more comfortable?

Does this sound like it is going to tie in beautifully with our follow-up strategy of the postcards, the phone calls, and so on? You are absolutely right. You meet people; connect with them meaningfully; write down something about their son, or their wife, or their situation, or their life; and you follow up.

Do not sell yourself at the meeting. If everybody introduces themselves and talks a tiny bit about their business, you can do that too. That is great—but just a *tiny bit*. But when you meet with people, meet with people not with a pitch. You are building relationships.

The other thing I will caution you about live events is to make sure that you are following up with people in a timely manner. If you let your leads get stale or if you let your name go by the wayside, then you have just wasted your time. You have wasted the effort of being at that event.

One more little side note that I read in the book *LinkedWorking* by Lewis Howes is to see opportunity in everyone. Don't preselect who you are going to talk to and who you are not going to talk to based on how they are dressed or if their market overlaps with yours. You never know who is one or two degrees of separation away from a seven-figure relationship with you, or a six-figure relationship with you. You never know, so try not to prejudge. You can be smart about it, but try not to prejudge.

Build relationships. And then, as you build that relationship a little deeper, it comes naturally to ask more about business details.

Set a goal for one live event a quarter—or maybe even one a month!

Online List Building

One more strategy is online list building. This is another way to add to your prospect list, your circle of influence. I love to do this—to offer good bait that makes people raise their hands and say, "Carrie, I want to do business with you or I at least want to know more about what you have to offer."

I refer to this as Magnetic List Building. The reason I call it that is because I always prefer to draw people to me. I would rather attract and not attack, something I learned years and years ago. It has a much better stick rate. It is a much better relationship if they come to you willingly instead of you tackling them or chasing them down. I think I learned that in fifth grade with boys. (Shhh, please don't mention that to my mom.)

You can make list building online as simple or complicated as you want to. But basically you set up a squeeze page or an opt-in page like you see at BlogBarefoot.com or that pops up at BarefootExecutiveTV.com or any other site that asks you for your name and your e-mail in exchange for information. You will be asking them for their names and their e-mail addresses in exchange for "free" information.

"Well, Carrie, I don't have any information." Sure you do. You could teach fifteen minutes of your best stuff. For example, you could give away an article or an e-book or a video.

Look at the sites I just gave you as suggestions. You probably see two or three squeeze pages a day when you are surfing the Internet. What can you offer in exchange for their information? That makes them a warm lead.

Social Media

If you are not involved in social media online, no matter what your business model, then you are missing out on a wealth of prospects, leads, and referrals.

Don't be overwhelmed by all the different sites. I like to focus on the "fabulous four." And chances are, you are already involved in at least one of these sites. I like to focus on LinkedIn, YouTube, Twitter, and Facebook.

You are going to build relationships in those groups. In Facebook and LinkedIn you can find groups of people who are like-minded, and you work that the same way you work a live event. You offer content. You offer connections. You have conversations with people and then people will be curious about your business and what you are doing. Be authentic and be real, and don't go into the group pitching, selling, or being "that guy." You know who "that guy" is, and you don't want to be that person.

So use social media. Twitter—a really powerful function—is http://search.twitter.com. Look for keywords. Look for who is having conversations about things that relate to your expertise. And look for groups to join on Facebook. You would be surprised at how many groups with how many thousands of prospects there are for you. Get involved in the conversation. Get established with relationships with these people.

LinkedIn—find a group or start a group. Start a conversation. Have some virtual events. YouTube—post videos with great content, short videos that are helpful to people.

If you are unsure about what to do with video or how to add that into your marketing mix, go to my free blog. Videomagnetism.com has a ton of free videos and resources that you can check out about how to add video effectively.

Social media has hundreds of thousands, and actually millions, of people there every day. You just have to find the right pond to fish in and be using the right bait.

What Could You Offer as a "Bribe" or "Bait"?

Then how do you follow up? I have some automated e-mails in place—e-mail newsletters, e-mail campaigns, articles—things that go out even without me touching them, where I follow up and offer more of my goods, products, and services.

Or I just educate them a little bit more about me. Maybe I refer them to some videos. Maybe I send them to some audios. Maybe I send them to some customer testimonials. Whatever it is, it is another way to draw people into the fold, to get them onto your list, and to be marketing to them over and over. Our goal is to get them on a list—either a snail-mail list, a phone list, a customer list, or an e-mail list. People fall into three different categories—e-mail people, mail people, and phone people. And only when you can touch people in all three ways can you keep them coming back for more and more.

Your Turn

List some things you could use as "bait."

_____

_____

_____

_____

PART FIVE RECAP

Who Wants What You Have?

No matter how great your product or service is, you have to know who wants it. You need to know that a buying population exists.

- Does your market have money? Do they have income to spend?
- Are they reachable online or off?
- Can you get to your market, and can they find you?
- Is there pain you can solve for someone?

Ideas to Income

Entrepreneurs have no lack of ideas. As a matter of fact, ideas are almost our curse. The key is to follow a plan or system for taking your ideas into implementation and then to income.

My suggestions:

- Qualify your ideas based on your motives and priorities.
- Identify potential obstacles, roadblocks, and discouragements.
- Name the benefits of moving your idea to action. Be specific.
- Be accountable to your spouse (or even better, your kids).
- Break your idea into action steps, about five at a time, so you're not overwhelmed with the overall picture.

Where Will They Find You?

Be online or be invisible. That's the hard truth for where we are in this technology age. Your audience lives on social networking sites and does extensive research online before buying. You must also be there.

Building Your Audience

From name and e-mail capture to social media friending, there are ways to corral your audience so that you can continue the conversation with them. I like to break this down into the four Ws:

- *Want them*—know who you want and why you want to serve them.
- *Woo them*—this is the courting phase, the "dating" segment of the relationship.
- *Win them*—make them an offer; come through on the problem you're solving for them.
- *Wow them*—surprise and delight them; over-deliver on their expectations and they will stay with you for life.

Where Will You Find Them?

- *Offline*: live business events, trade shows, industry conferences, and networking groups
- *Online list building*: name captures on your blog, swapping articles with other topic-specific publications, blogs or other sites, paid advertising
- *Social networking*: joining or leading niche-specific groups and discussions

Conclusion

The more I committed to doing things I loved to do,
the more the world stepped up and allowed me to
create a career that I love. Has it been easy, seamless,
sheer bliss? Not a chance. It's been work. And, it's not
always pretty.

—Jonathan Fields, *Career Renegade*

"Conclusion" doesn't really seem appropriate since I'm of the belief that business growth is a really dynamic process. Much like our "why" changes, our environment, our kids' ages, the stages of our lives, and our hopes change too. You can't ever be "done," or you start to die off the business growth vine.

I'm not trying to wax philosophical, but I believe too often we are sold the tale that "if you do this, *then* you can stop." For instance, if you go on this diet, *then* you'll be your goal weight. The reality is, we're in learning and action mode all the time. I don't want you to believe that "now that I've read that book, I'm done and I can get busy!"

It really doesn't work that way. For you this might be a starting point, or maybe this is a reinforcement of what you've previously learned or suspected. Great! Maybe this is an entirely new world to you, and much like I was at age twenty-five—a new mom, desperately reading everything I could get my hands on at the library—you aren't really digesting it all yet, but still just seeing what resonates and sticks.

I read dozens and dozens of books and ideas at that stage of my life. One phrase stuck with me, which led me to that first business. I kept studying, researching, learning, and excelling in what I did. Then another phrase from an article jumped out at me, gave me an idea, and I was off and running. I kept studying, researching, learning, and excelling in what I did. Lo and behold, at a live event, a theme jumped out at me and I was compelled to take action again.

My point is this: Take action, absolutely—but also keep learning and growing. Don't ever be finished. My recommended reading list and resources that I use actively in the growth of my business are located at BarefootExecutiveResources.com. I keep that list on a live page so that we can change and modify and add to without it being permanent as in a book. The Web is a dynamic and growing place, and we want to keep up with the times and trends!

As I'm wrapping this up, I'm more than a little distracted by the sound of tiny birds crashing into my office window. This has been going on for weeks and weeks. It's not cold outside. My windows are not especially clear; they have wooden blinds. And the birds don't seem to learn from their mistakes. They are doing the same thing over and over and over again and expecting to get to the other side of the glass pane.

They must be hurting, frustrated, stressed-out, and confused. I can't even imagine the bruises they are sporting. But I know that while they are trying harder and harder—and determined to never give up—they will never reach their goal.

Sometimes repeatedly doing what seems to be the logical thing isn't the logical thing at all. I encourage you to step back from the glass, to look over it, around it, under it, and beyond it, and see if you can find a different way to achieve your dreams.

That is what being a Barefoot Executive is about. Your life. Your dreams. Your way.

Acknowledgments

My mom said I had several books in me, and I've always taken for granted that someday I would write one. Much like the phrase "objects in the mirror are closer than they appear," however, writing a book is much more difficult than it seems.

So thank you to Joel Miller and the team at Thomas Nelson for seeing potential in *The Barefoot Executive* and recognizing that the hopes, dreams, and securities of people have shifted in a mighty way. The editors were very patient with me, and I'm grateful.

My parents are mostly to blame for this book. They convinced me from a young age that I could do more and be more. I will always remember Dad saying, "Carrie, if you ever figure out how to make money for talking, you'll have it made." (I did it, Dad!)

The teasing and torture that came with being raised alongside three brothers helped shape me to do business without gender bias or fear. The boys still aren't sure exactly what it is I do, but they're pretty sure I'm good at it. Brian, Kevin, and Robert, I love you.

My high school English teachers, Jan Neely, Shara Fox, and Molly White, thank you for insisting on writing and rewriting and rewriting.

To countless blog readers, podcast listeners, social media friends, and my amazing clients, thank you for believing in the Barefoot Executive—both the person and the lifestyle. You are the reason I keep shouting from the rooftops.

Thank you to the very special people in the case studies who took the time to share their experiences with me and gave permission for the use of their stories—and the readers of *The Barefoot Executive*.

And finally, for my husband and children—I never would have dreamed that an adoption would lead to career abandonment and then to business development and a life that we never had dared dream of. Thank you for being so unselfish with my time and energy. Thank you for always believing in the "next step." You are, and always will be, my "why."

About the Author

From corporate life to teaching high school to sales; to information marketing, consulting, and even providing virtual service, Carrie Wilkerson has been there and done that professionally and personally. As the "Barefoot Executive," Carrie Wilkerson has quickly become the definitive resource for helping others achieve extra income and career goals while working from home and keeping their priorities intact. She is a mentor/coach/advisor to more than one hundred thousand men and women through videos, podcasts, masterminding, mentoring, and live speaking. She is not only a business expert but also an expert *in* business.

Carrie's work-at-home methods have inspired thousands and have earned many awards, online and off. She has been featured in *Success at Home* magazine and the *Financial Times* (UK) and was named as one of the Top 5 Women to follow for Business by *Forbes*. She represents Google as one of five official Google Online Small Business Experts for 2011. She has received influence awards via Squidoo, *Entrepreneur Woman*, and the *Washington Post*-featured iPhone apps. She is a sought-after speaker and has shared the stage with many of her longtime idols, including John C. Maxwell, Zig Ziglar, Les Brown, and Andy Andrews.

Her passion is in teaching others to fill their stadium with fans so that marketing is easy and business is abundant. To connect with her, visit BlogBarefoot.com and BarefootExecutive.TV for schedules, details, and strategies.

Carrie lives in Texas with her husband and four childen.